D0886813

SPOOK

AND

OTHER

STORIES

BOOKS BY DAVID HENDERSON

Covey Rises and Other Pleasures
Sundown Covey
On Point
Spook and Other Stories

SPOOK

AND

OTHER STORIES

Tales of a Bird Dog

DAVID HENDERSON

Illustrations by Shep Foley

Lyons & Burford, Publishers

© 1995 by David H. Henderson
Illustrations © 1995 by Shepard H. Foley
ALL RIGHTS RESERVED. No part of this book may be reproduced in any manner without the express written consent of the publisher, except in the case of brief excerpts in critical reviews and articles. All inquiries should be addressed to: Lyons & Burford, 31 West 21 Street, New York, NY 10010.

Printed in the United States of America

10 9 8 7 6 5 4 3 2 1

Design by Catherine Lau Hunt

Library of Congress Cataloging-in-Publication Data

Henderson, David H.
    Spook and other stories : tales of a bird dog /
Dave Henderson ; illustrations by Shep Foley.
        p.   cm.
    Includes bibliographical references.
    ISBN 1-55821-402-X (cloth)
    1. Bird dogs—North Carolina—Biography.
    2. Henderson, David H.   3. Fowling—North Carolina.
I. Title.
SF428.5.H39   1995
799.2'34'092—dc20
    [B]   95-10778
                                                    CIP

For HERBERT and ALICE (SKIPPY) JENKINS

*In great affection, for I have hunted with him lo these
many years in the coverts of eastern North Carolina,
and indeed in the coverts of my mind when, out of
season, I remember the excitement and challenge
of quail hunting with my favorite cousin.
A lot of my stories I stole from Herbert.
And Skippy has hosted and fed me,
and lovingly put up with my warts and deficiencies,
but shared her poesy, for at least forty years.*

*And for PATRICK,
youngest grandchild at age eight, who offers me a
new beginning at trying to teach hunting, fishing,
and especially outdoor ethics.*

Contents

Introduction

Spook was truly, semantically and factually, as you shall see, an illegitimate SOB. But, along with Owen Wister's Virginian, when I say that, I smile. (No one reads Wister anymore, and euphemisms are passé—just *say* it!) This is not just a story of an old man and his now-dead dog, what Steve Bodio refers to as a "my old dog died today" story. Yes, that's part of it, but this little book is also a reflection of more than half a century of quailbirds and bird dogs, and kids, and pups, and bird hunters, and triumphs and disappointments. Some are certainly "twice-told," it being in the nature of bird-hunters to regale any sitting audience with dog lore, so I have often recited or written about these subjects, including the saga of Spook. Old men tend to repeat themselves. I hope that the old-fashioned word "love" shows through, because, as Rupert Brooke once poetized, "These have I loved." This is not then a requiem but a celebration of bird dogs. True, the protagonist may be the special dog, Spook, but he only crystallizes the memories. He is a symbol of the sport, a marker for dogs to come, and truly, while he was with me, one of the great ones.

Here are stories of the incomparable Spook, his successors, and of course his boss, a role assigned, fortuitously, to me. Perhaps "incomparable" is too strong a word. It is just that out of all the dogs that lived here during the great bird-hunting years, this near-white, dignified, and ultimately grand old setter seems most to deserve such accolades. For inas-

much as the Creator invested bird dogs with a shorter life span than man's, then within the life of a man there comes one dog, then another, and another. They are the players upon our stage, and as Gielgud is followed by Burton, and Burton by Jacobi, so in our play the characters are ever-changing. The play is essentially the same. But Spook was the first hero of a new work written for this player in my fortieth year. The drama was entitled *Birdhunting*.

By the time you read this book, I will have passed my eightieth birthday. I fired my first shotgun at about twelve under the auspices of Walter Mitchell—broad, black, and formidable—who was kind enough to take me rabbit hunting and to persuade my dad that I could use his 12 gauge without killing myself.

There were my first thirty or so years, when school, the Air Force, a law practice, marriage, and babies excluded pat 'ritches, as our old folks in the South called quail. Nor was there any special dog or dogs, although as a country boy I had lived among all sorts of canine companions. I was city-born but reared on a farm near the burgeoning city of Charlotte, in North Carolina, a state that we schoolchildren lauded as "The Old North State." There was a song by that title, and it was rendered loudly, if imperfectly pitched, in every North Carolina grammar-school room at least once a week.

Our loyalties were first to the state, next to the South, and only last to the nation. "Battle Hymn of the Republic" was not sung at our graduations. My Grandfather Jenkins for the last sixty years of his life would not wear a blue shirt, suit, or tie. Threatened by Yankee invaders, he at twelve years of age was forced to hide with the farm horses in the swamps. He was my idol, and to him I owe my love of the land. I hope I escaped or outgrew his prejudices.

As for me, living on the farm, I learned respect for people and property (separating what was mine from what belonged to a neighbor) and the differences between men and animals. Not to say that animals deserved, or got, less respect. But we raised and butchered beef, plucked and sold chickens, raised rabbits for market. And we hunted. None of this was done with malice, and no country kid ever pulled the wings off flies. Our ethic was that of farm folks everywhere, and I see no need for apologies.

After *our* war, that is, World War II, I found myself invited, from time to time, to duck-hunt or quail-hunt. I had no proper gun and was reduced to shooting with something or other borrowed until I bought the 16 gauge Remington '58 and in an excess of ignorance sent it back to the factory and had a "polychoke" installed. Now, varying choke devices have flooded the market of late, and some of the gun books I review have good things to say about them. I must confess, however, a touch of avarice at the time—I was simply trying to get all things for the price of one. Ducks and geese were still around, both locally in the creeks and at Currituck or Mattamuskeet. I would put the poly on modified and fire away from some stick blind on open water, or try to swing on a hot-tailed dove; tighten her up and knock down a Canada, provided I could shoot under the wing and not full-on. Then, if somebody suggested pat 'ritch, he'd have the dogs, and I'd select improved or open choke and try busting a covey with no real knowledge of "pick a bird."

It was in the midst of these shenanigans that my brother Wes moved heaven and earth to identify and find and marry Peggy, his dream girl, whose uncle, or some such relative, was one Skinny Warrington. Familial relationships being established by marriage, Skinny saw fit to invite me on a few legitimate bird hunts. Legitimate because he had honest-to-gosh Pointers that knew what it was about, and who, or rather which (they being dogs and not people), pointed, backed, and retrieved. (Note: Because it is almost impossible to write about bird dogs without anthropomorphizing, I'll most often use "who" instead of the more grammatical "which.") I remember we worked some territory near the little crossroads of Waxhaw (an area wherein I later spent years at the sport) and found pat 'ritch by the covey. It was a revelation, and I was hooked.

· 1 ·

The Conception

---

*A*fter the war, I fell into the practice of accepting every hunting invitation offered and thus met new friends and learned something about His Honor, Bob White. I might have referred to this earlier time as *before* Spook, but this would have shortened to B.S., so in flashbacks I'll talk about P.S., or pre-Spook.

I'm not sure how I met P.B., formally Pearl B. Beachum. I think it was because our wives were members of the same book club. Certainly it was well before he was raised to the bench. Flat, hard, and athletic in those days, he was about five feet ten inches, weighed in at maybe 165, and loved to quail-hunt. He did not care to be called Pearl, even when he attended Davidson College. Nor did one challenge him. He was, in the early 1950s, a weapons instructor for the Federal Bureau of Investigation, and the Winchester Model 12 was his favorite quail gun. He also owned bird dogs. At that time, I expect he was the fastest shot around (although I was a tyro, and everybody shot better than I). He gave exhibitions, blowing up grapefruit and blowing out candles. His favorite trick he showed off one afternoon on the flat top of my boat house. Leaving the Model 12 open on the deck, he hand-threw two clay pigeons, stooped, picked up the gun, and broke both before they hit water. Pretty impressive.

"Look here," he said later, "you face the water and throw a target; I'll face you and shoot overhead, trigger up." Well, he made good on that and called on me. "Hey, now you try it." We'd both been sipping the bubbly a bit, so I declined, but under pressure of the distaff audience looking on, took a turn. By golly! I hit the bugger. Unfortunately, I never could kill quail that way.

Years later, P.B. was appointed a district judge and struck terror on evildoers and their lawyers. He figures prominently in this recitation and is still a great friend. It was Beachum who, one spring day, took me "out to see the pups." One of those was Spook, who graced my dog lot for the next fourteen years.

The seemingly uncomplimentary characterization of Spook's genealogy in the opening paragraph of the Introduction was really accurate, and had it been naturally come by— that is, without interference from man—would undoubtedly have been just another minor scandal. Spook's mother was kept by John Collins for her owner, the aforementioned Judge Beachum. The putative (and, I have been led to believe) true biological father was a traveling man, fortunately not of the pejorative sense the term was used in the Joe Miller joke book, but simply a high-blooded male Setter being shipped to Pennsylvania to a new owner. He was scheduled to be held overnight at the Collins kennels, which figured heavily in the following years' activities chronicled here.

The Judge had substantial pride in the bitch, Pat, she being directly of the Sport's Peerless line bred by a pharmacist named Dr. Bobbitt in nearby Winston-Salem. Sport's Peerless had won the National in about 1939, but there had come along several generations, including that of Sport's Peerless Pride, and never a really bad descendant. Some months ago I obtained, courtesy of *American Field*, a poster picture, in full color, of Sport's Peerless, and out of respect for old Pat and her progeny, I have it hanging on my den wall. I do not know her dam, but Beachum's bitch must have been strongly Laverack in conformation, because the old lady had the large head and heavy dewlaps and thews, only a part of which genes were passed to Spook. In the family tradition, she was no field-trial racehorse, but one helluva good bird dog. In researching an article on Setters recently, I visited the old judge, and there on *his* den wall was a picture of Sport's Peerless, facing north instead of south, like mine, but still evidence of his acceptance of what I have sometimes chided him about—that Pat was the only good bird dog he ever had (which is not true, of course).

The transient, whom I'll call "Ghost" out of deference to his male line (but whose papers I never saw), was held in an adjoining or possibly a nearby pen. His forebears were as noteworthy as Pat's, at least on the male side. He was a direct descendant of Eugene M, who once won the National, and of Eugene's Ghost, of the Bird Dog Hall of Fame. He was nearly white and rode high at both ends, looking on point like a clipper ship, full-rigged. This line showed unmistakable Llewellin breeding, with finer features, and fortunately the pups took more after Daddy.

The timely juxtaposition of Pat's estrus and the overnight stay of Ghost brought about a happy union for the humans involved, and I presume for the participants. Ghost may have been delayed in shipment, but he certainly left the premises within forty-eight hours. I never saw him again, but I am greatly indebted.

You see, sometime during the darkness of night,

Ghost went over the fence. Asked whether there was human aid, support, or even encouragement, the Judge simply gives an enigmatic smile worthy of the Mona Lisa, and says, "Let's talk about something else, David." John Collins, in whose trusteeship was the Ghost dog, professed to his dying day, "Boy, I don't know anything about what you're talkin' about. Do you think I'd let a client's dog, with all those papers, ever get loose, much less breed to a friend's bitch without his payin' a stud fee? You oughta be ashamed for even intimating such a thing." And he would give his little crooked grin. The offspring were to a pup almost all white. Now, would a respected member of the judiciary *still* not tell the whole story? I'll never press. You see, he gave me two of the pups. And one of them was Spook. I never again heard of the others.

· 2 ·

A d o l e s c e n c e

Our youngest, the boy D.L., must have been about ten when I brought home two white Setter pups with light tan markings on head and ears. I had first seen them in the kennel at John Collins's, and the larger pup's brilliant white, which stood out in the darkness of the whelping box, together with his ancestry, immediately earned him his call name. Obviously, he was never registered, though I fancied the name Eugene's Peerless Spook. The slighter pup, being the runt of the litter and lowest in the pecking order, was dubbed Deuce. Since he was not long with us, I need only tell how pitiful he looked at ten weeks, peering through the fence, shivering and shaking uncontrollably with what was then called "chorea" and is now recognized as a symptom of distemper rather than as a disease in itself. After their shots, both youngsters had adverse reactions, and we thought to lose them. Deuce didn't survive. Spook did, but he always had a weakness on his left side which showed when he was tired.

I had built the dog pen back of the house on Radcliff in my first venture into owning my own quail-finder. Spook succeeded to residence following Frank, a papered Pointer out of Statesville breeding—possibly Warhoop Jake, as I recall. He certainly had field-trial capabilities, and I called him Next County Frank. I was never able to handle him, to some degree out of ignorance, but mostly because he wasn't bred for walking hunters. This week some dog psychologist issued a news release in which he stupidly attempted to generalize a list of "smarts" in the dog kingdom. Pointers were so far down the list that my newspaper didn't even list them. But this man didn't know old Frank.

Frank had three insatiable desires: for the chance to hunt quail in distant coverts, for a dalliance with some nearby representative of the opposite sex (not limited to the Pointer breed), and to be "out," i.e., not penned. Toward all three overlapping goals he devoted hours of thinking and planning, visible to the observer as the dog sat at the gate to the pen and cogitated. To be out he undoubtedly associated with each of the other ambitions. First he chewed the gate, then a nail-studded gate. Next it was over a six-foot fence. Then, when a horizontal "lip" on the fence was constructed, one could see him looking upward, changing position, looking up again, and, at the weakest spot, rising vertically to seize the chicken wire in his teeth, swinging happily until it collapsed, and so over the fence to freedom. I have told elsewhere that he finally climbed a large pine inside the pen, walked out on a horizontal limb, and jumped. He always returned, and I'd find him lolling relaxedly in front of the gate, a beatific smile on his face, when I came home from work. He reminded me of the famous Springmaid ads: "a well-spent buck on a Springmaid sheet." I sold him to a South Carolina hunter looking for a Jeep-hunting dog that "ran big." So Spook came to follow Frank.

I was finishing off the playroom interior with juniper planking, and used some of it to build a new dog box. That waterproof wood (used Down East for boat-building) furnished quality quarters for Spook for as long as he lived. It was "take-down," because in one piece it must have weighed three hundred pounds.

It became my first training venture, which I later often repeated, the puppy training of Spook as a working dog. Of course I had read Wehle and Wolters and Long, or whoever was writing training books at the time, and we stumbled through a thousand "sits" and "stays" and standard yard training. He was a willing, if not genius, pupil. I recall the day when, at about five months of age, he was running free in the yard and wouldn't come in. Whether or not you approve, I carried then a rolled-up newspaper as attention-getter. Cornered on the terrace, Spook met with loudly laid-on reminders of bossmanship that he never forgot. Seldom thereafter was calling in a problem. The children had their Beagle and a succession of other house pets, so Spook and I were free to go one on one, and thus bond for the duration. He was *my* dog.

· 3 ·

T r a i n i n g

---

*W*helped in late winter, Spook's rapid growth and home-training progress fed my hope of hunting over him in the fall of 1962 or 1963. Dates escape me, though the events of the past loom crystal clear. I inquired around for some qualified dog man to take the youngster for serious training. How lucky can boss and dog be? I found R. B. Patterson, some twenty miles away in the north end of the county.

I never, over twenty years, left off calling him "Mr. Patterson." Some would have called him a millhand, which he certainly was, in that he was employed in the nearby Kannapolis Cannon Mills. But that was only a small part of the man. Living with his wife and daughter in a neat frame house behind Antioch Church, his backyard flowed downhill, carrying with it a succession of dog pens. Dirt-floored, they were scrupulously clean, and I recall that on my first visit I noticed no odor.

His avocation, which on occasion became his vocation, was handling bird dogs. Some were his own. One or two at a time were for owners who wanted serious daily hands-on breaking. The semantics involved—breaking versus training—is important. A dog returned from Patterson was either to be given away or it was "broke." To the uninitiated, mention of the practice of "breaking" a dog might conjure up visions of beating the spirit out of a pup to command absolute blind obedience. Most bird-dog owners would whip any trainer using such tactics on their dogs. No, we simply use the term "broke" to mean that the dog is ready for quail hunting in all its aspects without bringing embarrassment to itself or its owner. Ready to find, point, back, and, with hope, retrieve. That sequence, it seems to me, goes beyond just "training."

Young Spook had already learned to ride in the car, finding at the end of a trip a delicious opportunity to break free. Before the day of traveling crates and other impedimenta, hunting dogs rode in the trunk of a car. I ordered and installed a periscopelike device that funneled fresh air into the trunk of the white Ford Fairlane that was rapidly evolving into a hunting and fishing car. So Spook popped in and off we went to school. Mr. Patterson said, "Just leave him in that second pen. I've yet to feed. Won't get to work him 'til tomorrow when I get off third shift. You come back in a couple of weeks and we'll see whether schooling that particular dog will be worth the money." Unlike training kennels where one plopped down a month's fee in advance—win, lose, or draw—here I was given a choice. No money now, come see what progress, if any, later, then perhaps talk of a second semester.

Led across a nearby broad broomstraw field on my first return, I saw this taciturn, gangly handler uncheck the trainee, give him a free run, whistle him in, and have him sit-stay. I saw a far better performance there than I had achieved in six months at home. On the month's end, I went back to see the pup point on planted pen birds. I had expected, in my naive way, to be entertained by a demonstration of the whole bit—point, back, and so on. It was not that way with Mr.

Patterson. Quietly he said, "I think this 'un will do. Take him home, put him in wild birds, and my guess is he won't need no further work." On that thirty days of contact with this paragon of breaking excellence, the career of a fine bird dog began.

Hunting with my neighbor and fellow lawyer Bob Sanders on Thanksgiving Day that first season, Spook picked up and retrieved a bird. A week later, hunting with Beachum along the South Carolina line below Waxhaw Creek near the telephone tower, the young fellow pointed, stood, and retrieved from across the road in veteran fashion. I felt like a new daddy!

Thus it was that Judge Beachum and I began a ten-year, regular every-Saturday-during-season bird hunt. It was fitting that Spook was back with his dam, Pat, and later with other dogs from John Collins's kennels, and I with all the grand guys who hunted out of that base and others of the fraternity in which I was now promoted from pledge to full dues-paying member.

The Boss

B ut first, perhaps more about this old man and the way things were long before Spook and the all-my-own bird-dog kennel.

I was reared on Scalybark Farm, a hundred acres on the edge of a growing city. My father, a lawyer, bought the acreage in 1926, having, of course, no inkling, when he signed the purchase money note, of the coming Depression. He was farm stock, self-educated, and enormously proud. I can yet today remember the lines on his face at the thought of having to ask the note holder for time when 1929 knocked us down.

I say "us" because I never heard him use the possessive "mine." Whatever he had was "ours" until the day he died. For good or bad, we, the family, were a unit. It is a precept I've tried to pass to my children and grandchildren.

When he moved us back to the country from the fine house in town, he was seeking for his kids a view of, and participation in, country living. I'm sure he wanted us to have to do some work in the fields, to learn about and be around livestock, and to shoot a shotgun. I was twelve at the time. Both mother and father being adamant about our getting an education, my siblings and I were sent back to town, to city schools presumably offering higher academic standards. But that did not bring relief from country chores, and in summer we were charged with everything from road-building to haycropping. He populated the farm with all manner of live things: a small goat, three real deer, peacocks, ducks, geese, turkeys, and the ubiquitous rabbit hutches, where I could not feed as fast as they bred.

All was not work. There were cherry trees to climb, a creek to dam up for a skinny-dipping swimming hole, weenie roasts, watermelons, and all manner of new adventures like hog-killing and calf-breeding. Obviously, the educational advantages my father sought as a supplement to formal schooling he provided in the environment.

As for the shotgunning, we were not a quail-hunting family. Our only dogs were the part-Collie yard dogs distinctive to all farm families. Squirrels abounded, and against the wily woodsman I sportingly used a Browning .22, loaded, you may remember, through the stock and holding sixteen shorts and fewer longs. I don't recall that long-rifle cartridges existed. Crows were anathema to farmers, being accused of everything from pulling up corn to stealing eggs. In fact, on one occasion Dad was chastising one Rob, who lived on the place, about Rob's possibly stealing eggs from the farm turkey nests, made in the woods. "Nawsir," said Rob. "It was one o' dem' black crows whut stole dem aig." "Yes," said Dad, "and I know what black crow that was!" But Rob was vindicated when one of the culprits boldly ran off the turkey hen, drove its bill into an egg, and flew away with the prize held high, presumably gulping the contents *en route*.

Our municipal police sponsored a crow hunt back of our place, and from dynamite to fifty shotguns wreaked havoc on a giant roost, leaving hundreds dead on the ground. The thousands of crows that came in at nightfall from the four corners were suddenly no more. I was too young to protest, nor do I know if I would have. It only struck me later that this was a useless massacre.

But the shotgun was ever-present for the raiders of the chicken houses—the possums and mink. And for an occasional wild-dog pack that worried the cattle. Once, Dad blew off the head of a copperhead coiled at our back door.

My publisher, Nick Lyons, prompted me to go reread Faulkner, whose stories of Mississippi make you see and feel what was happening, as distinguished from my tale-telling. Although I will never be Faulkner, I contrived a little story of my first rabbit hunt at the farm, with maybe, just maybe, a hint of Yoknapatawpha County.

· 5 ·

The Hunt (After Faulkner)

---

*I*t was cold in the predawn winter morning. Cleo softly tossed a pebble against the boy's window at the Big House. With window raised and wind whipping his nightshirt, the boy shushed his wake-up caller. Cleo said, "Git up an' git yo daddy's gun. We's gonna finish what we sta'tted yistiddy. Don't git no birdshots, neither. Hurry. We be's behind the big barn."

The boy's excitement almost made him pee in the long johns he was pulling onto his pipe-stem legs. Sneaking downstairs, fumbling in the closet under the steps for the old rabbit-eared Johannsen 12 gauge and a handful of his daddy's #6's, he grabbed a cold biscuit and let himself out the kitchen door. He did not lock it; there had been no key during his lifetime. He had to stop to retie his bootlaces, which were always likely to trip a thirteen-year-old country boy.

The barn loomed in the semidarkness, the smell of manure and hoss piss and steaming cows marking its location. Behind, Big Walter massed his troops. "You got de gun, boy? Lemme see. You don' wanna miss, an' you don' wanna cripple—you wanna kill th' sumbitch this time." Walter was wearing his big white cowboy hat, as usual contrasting with his bright black face and highlighting his gold-tooth smile. He mounted his old Iver-Johnson single barrel over his right shoulder. Rob, one of Walter's wife's nephews, spoke up. "I—I ain't got no gun, but I got my thowin' stick. I hittem side de haid, he gonna be plum daid." Egg (that was the only name

the boy had ever heard for the tall, gangly twenty-year-old)
popped in, saying, "I got this here hickory pole I done cut, an'
it'll sho' stop whatEVER I lay it on." Cleo bragged, "I gonna
run him down an 'ketch 'um by th' hin' legs."

Walter spoke, his deep bass voice growling orders.
"Now you boy, be keerful wi' dat gun, lessen yo' daddy kill
me. We gon' fin' dis fellow still in he bed, an' you or me one
gonna make sho' he don' git away. Iffen he do, we have to go
home an' git de trackin' dawg. Den we mought git th' whole
fambly!"

Meanwhile, the prospective victim, unaware of the
conspiracy against him, snuggled back in his bed, shared with
two surviving members of the late-summer litter. He had
known fear from his escape the day before, when he had simply outrun two Beagles. But a quarter-hour later, the sounds
of approaching footsteps fell on his sensitive ears; remote but

undeniably threatening, they caused him to open one large, dark eye. He turned slightly to facilitate escape should that prove necessary. Male human voices mumbled against the wind, and the subject of the hunt uttered first a muffled snort, then a strange low-pitched grunt. It showed a trace of panic, a foreboding. Death was in the air.

Walter and company, emboldened by numbers and appropriately armed, followed a fence line down into a draw where the quarry's home had long been suspected to lie. It was now daylight, and Egg and Rob and Cleo were talking big about what they would do "iffen we spot he eye befo' he see us." Boy, quiet with anticipation, carried the big old gun, now charged with two of the #6's, at port arms. He was not to know for another ten years that carrying a weapon cross-chest was called "port arms." At the time, he carried the gun so because it was so long he could hardly manage it any other way.

The residence sought was not easily seen, masked as it was by briar and bramble, and screened by a thicket of sweetgum saplings. Suddenly the pressure on the inhabitant was too great. With a great leap he sprang from the bed, cleared the open doorway, and fled, his athlete's body kicking into high gear in the first three jumps. The boy, almost startled out of his wits, swung his weapon up on his skinny shoulder, squeezed shut both eyes, and pulled the front trigger, inadvertently slipping against the second trigger to give one unholy BANG! And to knock himself flat upon his underpadded butt. Ears still ringing, he righted himself to the sound of clapping hands. His co-conspirators were shouting and laughing and holding high the prize.

The boy had killed his first rabbit.

· 6 ·

The Boy

D.L. and I were riding the new pickup back from the farm almost twenty years after old Spook had left us. The Boy is now mangrown and father of Patrick, seven. There still is that original closeness between father and son that has blessed the relationship these forty-four years. We don't talk much, sometimes while hunting not a hundred words a day, but the rapport is unmistakably there.

"Hey," I asked, "Do you remember much about Spook?"

"Of course. But there was one happening that I bet I forgot to tell you. I was just sixteen, and you let me have the Fairlane and trusted me with the dogs. We had Spook and Mack. I picked up George and Stuart, and we went down after school to the Mobley Place. Those guys never did want to walk much, being city-bred, and I couldn't keep 'em going. So after awhile we sat down to rest—maybe smoke a cigarette we couldn't do at home. Suddenly I realized the dogs weren't with us. I knew you'd raise hell if they got lost, so I was on my feet in a hurry.

"You know where the old red house is on the right going down—that place with the thicket of briars and plums behind it. Well, I had a hunch, and followed it up, and sure enough, Spook was pointed and Mack backing. I moved in the way you and Judge Beachum had said, and kicked up a covey. I know I had the Ithaca 16 pump, and I fired twice and got two! Boy, you ought to have heard me holler. It was my first double, and I was as excited as I've ever been. I wonder that I never told you about it."

"Well," I said, "there was an earlier time. Beachum and I had decided it was time for you to get your first quail. You'd been following us around all the first half of that season and hadn't connected on a shot. But you were game and enthusiastic, so we conspired to skip shooting the next time there was a good point in open territory. We'd see what you could do if you weren't intimidated. We had already found a covey or two, but when we came up along Beachum Road, in a half-acre straw field I can still recall, there Spook stood solid in the middle of the field. Mack was backing, as usual. The judge told you to 'move right up,' so we lagged behind to let the kid have his shot. Only two birds flew. You fired and the one on the right fell, and we'd made a birdhunter! It was a memorable day for ole Dad."

I think it was that same year, probably near the end of February, that on a not-too-cold day, only D.L., the dogs, and I were hunting a mile or so south of where he'd gotten his first bird. It was near the place we called "Hawk Ridge" because some farmer kept hanging dead raptors on the fence beside the road. The dogs were working inside a wood line, down into a sort of valley or big gulley. Apparently they overran a single, because I know they were out in front of me toward the top. Suddenly I heard the flush behind me and turned just in time to see The Boy, who was trailing, swing the Ithaca on the bird's course, which was straight toward me. I had no time even to fall flat. Then I saw him lift off the

line of fire and there was no report, and this old man had great pride that his son had been taught that hunting buddies were more important than another bird. If I haven't thanked him, I now do.

· 7 ·

Pete

Strange how these memories pile up. It was about 1964 that first-daughter Shep sashayed in one day, having in tow a tall, rather nice-looking guy introduced as Pete Foley, soon-to-be lawyer. It was obvious to Dad that he was slated to be more than just a lawyer—something about the way she smiled. Not exactly hungrily, but . . .

Not wanting to have anything untoward slip up on me as family, I invited him to go birdhunting, a sure test of a young man's fitability at my house. "Know anything about bird-huntin'?" I asked. "Nossir," he said, not too respectfully. Well, he had been a Marine, and a law student, but he didn't know Billy about quail and bird dogs. However, he was game. I remember he, Shep, and I were on the back side of the Massey property, off the road that runs east from the birthplace of Andrew Jackson (as the South Carolinians contend). Late in the afternoon the dogs came in, except that Spook didn't show. It was a habit of his—this finding a sundown covey and staying right on the roost until I found *him*. We hollered and whistled and shot the gun but never could locate the dog, until he finally came to the car on his own. I had used the time to assess the young fellow, who, as darkness came on, certainly had better things to do with a pretty girl than help her old man look for a lost dog. I later determined that this was the apogee of his patience, his Irish blood demanding more than just waiting around. Shep said, "Dad, we're going to get married." No by-your-leave—just the conclusion. And Pete added, "And I'll call you 'Dave,' not 'Dad.'"

By the next season, then safely captured, Irish and all, he was following the dogs with us like a veteran. There was the day he, D.L., and I hunted the now well-recognized Beachum Road, it being sand-clay and running through the heart of the Heath-Massey property Beachum and I had bird-leased. I can recall every detail. The road ran east and west, and along the north side several openings, once cultivated, flanked the wood line, inside which the ground fell away smartly to a creek bottom some several hundred yards distant. Spook trailed off on an old logging road downhill, but didn't seem too sure of his quarry. Near the bottom, I stopped to take a breather. At the most inopportune of moments, the dog swung sharply right, a covey exploded, and I, caught with gun leaning against a tree, heard three quick shots. Knowing D.L. was as out of position as I was inhibited, I turned to Pete. Spook and Mack proceeded to pick up *three*. Three on a covey rise? I didn't know half a dozen old timers who could legitimately kill three on the rise. And here this tyro, this amateur, this fellow I'd only been teaching half a season—THREE on the rise! Damn!

· 8 ·

The Urge to Kill

---

*T*he bloodthirsty title to this piece comes as a realistic, not funny, drive that strikes a peace-loving man only rarely. I suppose it is part of being on a military mission, of having somebody rape your sister, or of somebody stealing your bird dog.

It happened once in the Spook days, and the white dog was at the peak of his prowess. As D.L. grew to manhood, he was rapidly becoming a fine bird hunter, and by the time he was seventeen or eighteen, I had no compunction about his taking truck, gun, and dogs to hunt our extensive bird-leases near Waxhaw. Sometimes he would take a buddy, but like his dad, there were occasions when either no partner was available or solitude beckoned. I have a great respect for solitude. It is a cathartic, a cleanser of the mind, and a healer of the wounds of the week. To be absorbed in nothing but the immediate environment is to slough off the trials and tribulations of living in today's world. So I encouraged the boy to practice a bit of onemanship on occasion.

I don't think that old folks ought to go traipsing around the woods alone. We are subject to all kinds of attacks, broken bones, lost return routes, and other accidents. Young hunters are also similarly exposed, but weren't we all once at the risk-taking age? And now how careful! At any rate, there came a day, or rather nightfall, when D.L. called home in a mood just short of panic. "Spook's lost," he said. My heart sank. "Where are you and what happened?" I almost shouted.

"I'm across from the Mobley Place, a quarter-mile north of the old Brown cabin, and I'll meet you at the intersection of the Indian Trail road. Come as quick as you can." I knew Spook was bad about staying stuck on a covey that had gone to roost, but on the other hand, he had never failed to show up within the hour. And in the area where he was lost, there were several paved highways that could prove deadly to a lost and wandering dog. I broke all records heading south the twenty miles from home to the named intersection. Spook's lost! *Lost* kept crowding my brain as I traveled, now in darkness, the old familiar road to our hunting territory.

It was at a time when attacks on laboratories doing research on animals for human benefit had just begun. The newspapers were full of stories about dogs, lost or boldly stolen, who were sold to the labs. But the animal rightists were compounding the problem counterproductively by destroying animal subjects. This created the need for replacements, and thus more pets and hunting companions were being funneled into the system. In my part of the country, every missing dog, registered or stray, was vulnerable to the threat of disappearance into the pipeline. This was what was on my mind during that seemingly endless trip.

Fishtailing to a stop alongside the truck, I found the youngster almost in tears. He was alone except for a gyp lying in the dog box. She had been the cause of all the trouble, or at least her conduct had created the situation wherein her bracemate was lost.

"Tell me again what happened," I asked. D.L. then related a sad tale. "I, Bess, and Spook were coming through that new-cut bean field behind the Brown cabin. She had smelled bird and was so feisty and unmanageable, I decided to take her back to the truck so she wouldn't flush that sundown covey I knew would be in the pocket where the briars meet the beans. I wasn't worried about Spook. I knew he'd find the covey and be locked in for the whole time it would take me to shut Bess up. She was a little trouble, but within fifteen or twenty minutes I was back expecting to see that white shadow right where the birds usually are. But he wasn't there! I blew the whistle, then hollered, then fired the gun. I hollered some more, followed the edge back up the way we had come, broke down into the bottom to look, but it was getting too dark to see anything. So I left my jacket where the truck had been parked and went to the store to call you—and, Dad, I— I'm just sorry!"

No need to place blame. What do you do when your lead dog just disappears in home and familiar territory? A veteran of a hundred hunting days within a mile of the site just doesn't get "lost" for very long. At least by next morning he's bedded down where you left a hunting coat or your shell vest. That night we had knocked on every farmhouse door along the road, leaving phone number and reward offers a mile each way. And only then, having left my Woolrich hunting shirt (the clothing that had been next to my body and therefore a hopeful magnet), had we headed back home, as disconsolate as two guys could be. Jack Daniels soured on my tongue.

I took off work next day armed with a handful of typed notices with my name and number, the dog's description, and a reward offer. Backtracking, I revisited the farmhouses, added a few, and struggled home as sad as the night before.

It was on the following Saturday, hunting alone (D.L. had basketball practice) with whatever else was in the kennel, but with a heavy heart, that I spotted the big harvest machine working the bean field next to where D.L. had last seen Spook. "Hello," I shouted to the operator, twenty feet above me. "You cut that adjoining field Wednesday. Did you by any chance see a big white Setter bird dog?" Came the reply that offered only a glimmer of hope: "Yep, I saw a fellow wearing a knit hat with a white dog on a string headed cross-country thataway." He pointed at a forty-five-degree angle from the road where we'd left notices. With gratitude bubbling in my throat, I thanked him, then took a sight line across a woods toward where another paved road lay a mile in that direction. Maybe, just maybe, there'd be some luck. At least the dog wasn't a roadkill!

Racing the pickup south, then at right angles along the road that would be intersected by my sight line, I pulled off to the shoulder, got out, took a deep breath, dropped two #6 shells, the heaviest I had, in the O/U, and placed the shotgun carefully, muzzle down, in the passenger seat. Only then, at about ten in the morning, did I begin a house-to-house search, alternating left to right. Before dismounting, I carefully eyeballed every backyard, chicken house, and dog pen from the road. If I couldn't see the back side of the place, I would drive into the driveway, wary all the time that the miscreant who had stolen Spook might come barreling out of the house with firepower. Lawyer-trained, I was, however, ignoring all the rules. I had not called the sheriff. I was there to get back my kidnapped friend and companion.

So, when half a mile from the intersection I spotted, behind a small frame house, old buddy Spook chained to a stake, I rolled out of the pickup, shotgun at hand. This, I thought, is the way folks being tried at my courthouse have killed somebody. Or worse, have come in to the emergency room with their guts blown out.

It is a matter of great good luck that no one was at home. Checking carefully that such was the fact, I quickly loosed Spook from the snaffle, noticed that the SOB had taken off my collar and substituted another (without a name, mind you), and clucked him into the seat beside me. Then we roared off. The Union County sheriff, of course, had no evidence, I having removed same when I retrieved the subject, as we say at the bar. Never mind. There was a happy reunion at our house when D.L. got home from school—and I realized that there are some things important enough to fight for. Spook was one of them!

Field Trials

There was a time in the mid-1960s when I dabbled in field-trialing. Spook was a walking birdhunter's dream so far as pace was concerned, so he never competed with the buzz-bomb streakers. I joined something called the Queen City Pointer and Setter Club, but with a limited string of dogs, I would usually hunt the big white Setter an hour or two before trial time, break off to watch the show and have lunch with the guys, check out the winners, and catch a sundown covey about dark. This meant that Spook spent a lot of time in the dog box, but he didn't seem to mind too much if he had been run a couple of hours in the morning. Later, when Rebel's Polly Who? joined our kennel, I'd devote the whole day to the contest and just leave Spook and Mack at home. But that is another story.

Trials were held across the railroad from John Collins's house, where the club had set up a backcourse and bird field. Around the old tenant house converted into headquarters were some big old trees, a dilapidated barn, well house, and a couple of sheds. Most owners parked under the trees and staked out the day's contestants in the shade if the event was early in the season and before the leaves fell. A visitor, as well as the participants, could thus see just about all the dogs that would be engaged.

During the several years I was a member, I never saw but one dog outside the Pointer and Setter breeds. That was the day somebody wanted to cause comment, so he brought a German Shorthair. No one expected him to win, place, or show—and he didn't! The tradition was then, and is now, too strong to accept the versatiles in this once-prime quail country. A few Brittanys are beginning to show up in some bird hunts because territories are now limited, and maybe I see them because I now have to favor short hunts and can no longer reach the far side of the bean fields. Yet—and I know this is treason—I have never seen a first-class working Brit on wild quail. I'm sure it's my loss, and the breed's champions will back their choice with real money, but only one non-Pointer/Setter was even entered in the National Bird Hunters' Association (NBHA) field trials in all of South Carolina last year. And that one didn't win *either*.

The Queen City functions were not sanctioned trials. That is, they were conducted under local rules that sometimes coincided with what are now NBHA standards, sometimes with the National Shoot to Retrieve Association (NSTRA) regulations. I am not sure that either group was formally organized at the time. As best I recall, each brace was put down at the beginning of the backstretch, with two judges on horseback. Mounted observers followed the judges, and some walking folks came last. Owners and handlers were announced with a bullhorn, although almost all owners took their own dogs through. It was mostly a one-man, one-dog affair. Only a few present could have qualified as "professionals," and they were usually from a group that might breed and sell half a dozen dogs a year, only one or two being "started," the euphemism for half-broke. Or perhaps a guy boarded a kennelful for somebody who lived in town.

On "loose your dogs," the judges watched as the

competitors flowed around an open field; compacted to pass through a narrow lane crossing a creek (where Judge Beachum's walking horse almost always had to be led across); climbed at a furious pace into a larger open area flanked by hedgerows, where planted pen birds could be found; and then moved back to the bird field in front of headquarters and the assembled wives, spectators, children, and hangers-on.

It was a time of great excitement when the front-running dog appeared in the bird field. In the distance could be heard the "hall-o-oo" of a handler, seeking sight perhaps of the second member of the brace still dallying in a briarpatch whence had already flown the quarry. Then the judges would appear, the slower dog come up, and there began the showpiece action before the assembled spectators.

While the trialers were on the backcourse, new pen birds had been randomly set out in the five-acre bird field, usually "put to sleep" by head-under-wing twirling sufficient to encourage a held position for fifteen or twenty minutes unless kicked up. Occasionally, a bird-placer would use a different technique, actually *throwing* a bird down hard from a Jeep. The befuddled quail seemed to remain frozen and certainly winded, for the most part, until the dogs, working frantically now and hailed on by the handlers, came to point and, with hope, to back appropriately. On a find, the lucky handler would raise a hand, the judges would observe for style, an opportunity would be given for the bracemate to come up, and a gunner would walk in, kick up, and shoot the flushed bird. Alternatively, the handler himself would flush, then pop the .22 blank pistol. In neither format was the dog held to standards of steady to wing and shot.

This stricter requirement, now held by some organizations, seems inappropriate to walking bird hunters who want the dog to watch birds down and move quickly to retrieve. It has always seemed to me to be an artificial point of argument, like how many angels can stand on the point of a pin. Adherents of one side or the other have no hope of cross-persuading.

These little field trials proliferated in the South, and in recent years I find that we were no different from folks in Wisconsin or Kansas or even New England in showing off our pointing dogs among friends and kin. There simply was no real organized national standard except for the big-time horseback Ames Plantation–type show. The success of the local activity was measured in network friendships rather than in silver loving cups. I must say that the few trophies still on my shelves bring back fond memories of times and people and places, and an occasional tear for a dog departed.

Our club had access to and used about 150 acres, flanked by a railroad track on one side. I recall that when the once-daily train was scheduled to pass, everybody grabbed up any loose-running dogs and the trial was delayed until the vanishing smoke indicated the danger had passed.

I made lots of friends at these gatherings. There were doctors and lawyers, farmers, pulpwood workers, filling station operators—all kinds and levels of economic standing tied together by a love of seeing finely trained dogs do what Pointers and Setters are supposed to do; that is, locate, point, back, and, off the course, retrieve.

Outstanding among new contacts were the friendships I developed with a pair of Lumbee Indians originally from Robeson County, North Carolina, and lured to our area by a desire to escape the poverty of that rural county. I recall a doctor overly active with his new electric collar and abusing one of his dogs until I threatened to use the collar on the owner. We did not part friends. But there was a tough landscape worker who always had impeccably trained dogs, and an earth-moving equipment operator who traded in bird dogs and never to his dying day learned the difference between truth and falsehood.

Even in the 1960s I knew trial judges wanted fast competitors to such extent that I wouldn't enter Spook. His Laverack bloodlines simply had not engendered in him the desire to engage in footraces. That was not his style, although he could move out to circle a bean field when it mattered. Today every commentator and outdoor columnist writing on the subject will tell you that the demand, at every level, is *speed*. In researching for articles in *Pointing Dog Journal* and other national magazines, I find that almost every handler I interview, including those competing in NBHA and NSTRA, acknowledges that the field trials don't match the needs of walking bird hunters. And as one active handler told me, "Beg your pardon, but you just couldn't make it these days." And after checking my aging and bulging waistline and watching him and his peers at a fall trial near Clover, South Carolina, I was convinced he was right, no matter the unsolicited put-down. The pace was breathtaking and bore no resemblance to a Saturday's bird hunt.

Here in the nineties, the activity has progressed to a more stable form. At Clover, the rules are established under the NBHA. Winners accumulate qualifying points for district, state, and, ultimately, national participation. The local club sponsor is part of a state organization with officers, standards, and periodic publication of coming events, winners, profiles, and interesting dog information. At this writing, I am advised that six or seven local clubs have established a North Carolina–sanctioned NBHA group. And the various national organizations are going full-bore to blanket the country, giving us all hope that bird dogs are still important.

Another sign of the times is the societal change that recognizes members other than the old-time male WASP. I have just seen my first black owner-trainer-member, which in South Carolina is great progress. And I watched as Vicki Homesley, a talented woman trainer, worked her puppies to the finals and the cup for puppy stakes. She has since duplicated that feat at the NBHA Nationals. Neither variance raised so much as an eyebrow, and all who paid their entry fees were welcome both in the runnings and in the lunch and social gathering that is always a part of the sport.

My daughter/illustrator Shep Foley and I recently attended one of the really big-time two-day regional trials of the horseback variety at Hoffman, North Carolina. Winners there go on to compete at the nationals at Grand Junction. Should you as a bird-dog enthusiast never have seen such a spectacle, make an effort. The dogs are speed demons, and handlers are entitled to spotters, also on horseback, to keep track of the competitors. Action is furious. The gallery is colorful. The sounds are exhilarating. In short, this is a unique experience you don't want to miss.

· 10 ·

Indian Territory

Spook and I had some memorable adventures in what I
call "Indian Territory." Geographically, I'm referring to
Robeson County, in the sandhills section of North Carolina.
Almost all the Atlantic Seaboard was at one time under the
sea, with two distinct fall lines. The westernmost is at the base
of the Blue Ridge Range of the Appalachians, dropping off
into what is known as the Piedmont (from the Italian, I suppose, for "mountain foot"), and the easternmost is at the
easterly edge of the Piedmont, known in our area as The
Sandhills, whence runs the coastal plain down to the Atlantic.

Currently before Congress, twenty-five years after
Spook, is still the question of official recognition of the cop-
per-skinned natives of the county. Are they or are they not an
Indian tribe? By state statute they have been named the
"Lumbees," a manufactured English word not related to their
original language. Students of linguistics identified that as
Siouan, a language of the Sioux, or Dakota, Plains Indians,
which have never been suspected of habitation in this area.

There is another mystery attached to these Native
Americans. Every history buff knows of the famous "Lost
Colony" of English established by Sir Walter Raleigh on
Roanoke Island off the North Carolina coast in 1594. And of
how Captain John Smith was detained while returning to
bring assistance to these beleaguered colonists until it was too
late. The English had disappeared, leaving only a carved code
word that was never quite translated. Now comes the sticker.

One John Lawson, billing himself in his writings as an English "Gent," traveled in 1710, more than a hundred years later, from Charleston westward across the Carolinas. In his peregrinations, he discovered at about what is now Robeson, Natives with gray eyes. Had he found the lost colony? Who knows, but my Lumbee friend Bobby Locklear spoke naturally with as near a Cornwall dialect as any resident of the Outer Banks. He said "Oi" for "I," and "hoigh" for "high," and otherwise ran the gamut in pronunciation. Unlettered himself, he could only have inherited this speech pattern.

But enough of ancient history. I had met Bobby and his buddy John Cummings at one of those Queen City field trials I once attended. Locklear bore a family name that, associated with Hunt, Oxendine, and Chavis, mark members of the Lumbee group. John was only half-Lumbee, his father having been Irish. I was initially impressed by Bobby's and John's bird dogs, predominantly all-white Setters. I learned that they had befriended a doctor in a neighboring county and acquired a pair of male Setters that were outstanding in appearance and performance. Later, I recall that at the doctor's death they got a brood bitch. They were always training puppies or running trials, or going back home to hunt wild birds.

I was a young lawyer making a name, I suppose, or at least making a living, engaged a bit in politics with a session in the state legislature under my belt, and a growing attraction to quail hunting. Spook was my lead dog. In any event, my economic standing was substantially above that of these new friends, who at some point invited me to go "down home" for a couple of days during season. Actually, I was

flattered to be thought one of the guys and perhaps a real birdhunter.

They seemed offended when I offered to stay at a nearby motel, stating positively that a married couple—cousins—expected me as houseguest. Sure enough, I settled in at the residence of Bake Locklear, his wife, and their two sons, one of whom gave up his bed in the modest brick bungalow. (When that boy grew up, he became the first Lumbee ever to be accepted at the University of North Carolina School of Medicine. How proud I was to have known him and his educationally insistent parents, both of whom taught school.)

I suppose I made all sorts of social errors in my efforts to obliterate any trace of the differences in standing. On the first day of hunting, I appeared with a pair of boots so old they bore patches on patches. I didn't want to appear a novice. Indian pride, however, saw it a bit differently. "Dave," Bobby said, "if you cain't affoird some better boots, we'll take you to the store and buy you some." Properly chastened, I went to the truck and put on my own new ones.

Bobby's daddy was not named Locklear but rather Goines, from which fact you may draw your own conclusions, but which was no matter of consequence in the community. He maintained a large lot full of deer- and foxhounds fed on offal from a neighboring slaughterhouse. Among the long-ears, however, was a badly beat-up lemon-and-white Pointer named Bo, who appeared to have tangled with a buzz saw at some recent time. "Only these Robeson briars," I was told. And that set the stage for Spook and me, the lemon Pointer, and the white Setters brought along by Bobby and John. I was to find that when you hunted with Indians, you hunted hard, your dogs hunted hard, and at the end both hunter and canine looked about like Mr. Goines's Pointer.

Strangers go not lightly into the bird field in Robeson County. It is axiomatic that one go attended or risk no return. And I speak as a veteran of the territory, and also as a lawyer familiar with the multiple criminal prosecutions from that area that bejewel the North Carolina Supreme Court reports. It is a country of love or violence, and I was fortunate to be loved. Not so much as was later lavished on my new little Setter Rebel's Polly Who?, but that is another story.

On this first of many trips, I learned what the dictionary means when it defines "swamp." The flat black soil of the countryside enables a train track through the community to go sixty miles without a curve. The low-lying cypress bays interspersed with highland swamps known as "pocosins" fill with water during wet seasons, and knee-high rubber boots are de rigueur. Deer proliferate, and raccoons, possums, foxes, and all manner of four-footed beasties, plus myriad feathered creatures, abound. Landowners are divided between white and Indian, and only your host knows when and where hunting is permissible. In addition to Bobby's and John's territory, I was able to wangle more hunting opportunities through some old acquaintances at the courthouse.

Our first encounter with the hunt as ordained by Bob and John became a pattern for other, similar jaunts: up at daylight on some frosty morning, breakfast with Bake's family before they rushed off to school, dogs and gear loaded into a pair of pickups. Then we three, with some nephew or other, would strike out for fresh territory. Mostly, Spook and I liked what is locally known as "flat piney woods"—open space under a canopy of mature longleaf pines with an understory of brown grass or other low-growing vegetation. At its best, this was home to the coveys we sought, offering fair shooting and some sighting of where the birds went. Walking was far easier than when we had to cross a creek-run with flanking green briars and canebrakes twice as high as a man's head.

I was shooting my Sweet Sixteen Browning with modified choke. This was possibly too tight for the terrain, but because this was in paper-case days, the plastic and shot-pouch had not further restricted the pattern. I recall shooting reasonably well, except on one occasion my guys never let me forget.

We had worked out a cut-over at the upper end of a bay, finishing at the edge of an open field of perhaps two hundred acres. Spook pointed in the honeysuckle thicket that marked a quail's last cover. Bo and the other Setters backed prettily. Sure enough, out flushed a single, and Ole Dave was in front, with a wide-open opportunity. So, before God 'n' everybody I threw *three* loads of #8s vainly at the bird. All missed! And I had to watch all the interminable time it took that critter to fly a quarter-mile in plain view to the next county with the laughter of my companions roaring in my reddened ears.

Those were wonderful days, with wonderful friends, a sufficiency of birds, good dog work, and an education in relationships. In 1994 Bobby Locklear died, and John looks not too well. I haven't heard about their dogs.

· 11 ·
Hot Wires and Cold Noses

The Robeson County hunts with the Lumbees went along for several years. The infrastructure of the county itself was an anachronism—way behind in education, economics, and race relations. It is unbelievable but true that in the thirties, Robeson was probably the only county in the world that had *four* separate school systems. There were, of course, white, colored (now black), and Indian buses, and a different bus for a group called "Smileys." As best I could tell from local discussion, a man of that name and indeterminate blood moved to Robeson from South Carolina, and his progeny were not only numerous but identifiable as "mixed blood."

When I hunted there, bitterness among the races was an everyday thing. I recall one night when I had been invited after a bird hunt to the home of a Lumbee who taught woodworking at an Indian school. It was a fabulous game dinner, with quail, barbequed rabbit, venison (about the legality of which I did not ask), and, I think, Brunswick stew, which meant there must have been squirrel as a required ingredient.

The teacher's son, a young man in his early twenties, began to express his frustration with, and indeed true hate for, the system. I was the only white present, and the situation was embarrassing. His topic, though, was the bus system, and I had to feel sympathetic. "Every morning," he said, "the white bus comes by, then the nigger bus, then the damned Smileys, before they pick up us Indians." But that night was not all disappointment, for the boy's aunt brought forth three huge scrapbooks detailing the life and times of Henry Berry Lowery, outlaw and patron saint of the tribe. I was there with the history, and a part of it, because the Lowery gang was buried in the cemetery lot alongside the Lumber River, and just outside the house where I was guest.

I tell you this because the rare acceptance this white man received was an integral part of the experience. Spook and I had been joined by Rebel's Polly Who?, a tiny tricolor Llewellin who was my pride, despite the favoritism I'd long shown for Spook. The Indians Bobby Locklear, John Cummings, and a boy named Les Taylor thought she was the fairest damsel in all of dogdom. And she was indeed a paradigm of excellence, both as a bird dog and as a lovable lapdog, given her propensity for crawling toward my heart at every sit-down.

How much did they love her? Once, when the temperature was below freezing and the chill factor down to zero, Miss Polly got caught and lost on the far side of Saddletree Swamp. We were hunting on lands belonging to the Biggs family, large landowners and professionals in the county, and I had wangled the invitation through my old courthouse buddy Murchison Biggs. We whistled, called, fired the guns— no response. Then we heard a faint bark or yip of the kind you've heard before, when your pup's check cord is caught in a fence out of your sight—a completely mournful wail. The water was cold and deep, and I sought advice as to how to drive around.

"No sir," said Les. "We might not find her. I know right now where she is." Whereupon with a wave of his hand he disappeared into the thickness of the swamp, crossed the running water that was up to his waist (and well above his leather boots), and in half an hour strode triumphantly back to the trucks carrying a tail-wagging, joyous gyp who was busy kissing his bearded face. And almost in unison they said, "You don't think we were going to go off and leave Polly?" Now what kind of love is that?!

Perhaps what followed was not fair to Murch Biggs, because of the social issues still unresolved in his county at that time. Biggs couldn't go to supper with us, but I asked him to arrange guest privileges for us at the Lumberton City Club, which he graciously did. I'm sure he didn't realize that John Cummings would tell me of his surprise at finding himself in this bastion of white supremacy. "David," he said, "when I left down here to go to Charlotte, white people sat on the main floor of the theater, and blacks and Indians had to sit each on separate sides of the balcony. I never believed I'd sit in the City Club." But we did, and I trust Biggs caught no flack. He'd been nice about the hunting permit.

On one occasion, passing through the yard of a deserted cabin where somebody kept free-ranging hogs corralled only by a single-strand electric fence, Spook found trouble. He was always wont to mark territory when on new ground. This time he elected to use the fence post as a marker. Now, water and electricity have an affinity for each other, and the voltage was sufficient to send him squalling to the truck. You can only imagine the shock to one's nearest and dearest when caught by lightning. I was sure he was ruined, at least for the day's hunt, but after a while he perked up and joined Polly with me.

The three of us were hunting the outside of a swamp

into which John and Bobby had earlier disappeared, looking for one of their dogs. A bit weary, I sat down on a stump to wait their return. I could hear them but not see them. My two dogs came up to wait with me. Suddenly old Spook, looking at his lovely bracemate, found himself in love. This state of affairs coming so soon after the encounter with the hot wire, I told my returning hunters about the incident. I also told them I wanted to go back by the cabin, where I intended to cut off and take with me a ten-foot strand of that wire. Might come in useful, I explained.

Those trips were physically hard on everybody concerned. At the end of two days everyone was exhausted. It was a sad sight to see Spook come up out of a drainage ditch soaking wet, almost in shock, but still dead game. No greater loyalty!

· 12 ·

The Setters

To know your dog you need to know his geneaology. Don't tell me. I'm sure your Uncle Ike had a dropper that was the best bird dog in the county and that he killed three hundred quail a year over him, or her. That he, she, or it would find, point, back, and retrieve. Well, no doubt there have been those great unknowns, but you couldn't sell one of them for the ten thousand or more currently paid by the Japanese, nor for the forty to sixty *thousand* reportedly paid for Flatwood Hank and brother a few years ago at Hoffman. Knowledgeable bird-dog men don't throw around that kind of money without a pedigree going back six generations or more. As I've written, Spook did not bear the heraldry of legitimacy, yet he turned out to be something like your Uncle Ike's paragon of excellence.

But I did have relatively believable word of mouth tying him to the Eugene line on the male side and the Sport's Peerless line for his dam. And his conformation reflected much of what I have since read about Setters in America. First, he was large by local standards, weighing perhaps seventy pounds versus an average of fifty to fifty-five for mature English Setter males. His head was large and majestic, looking almost Oriental when at rest, yet it carried no heavy thews or dewlaps. He was not wholly Laverack but had inherited both the finer muzzle and the soft temperament of the Llewellin.

I was once offered a thousand dollars for him when

good broke dogs were four or five hundred, but I told the banker who wanted him that he didn't have enough money. Spook was the epitome of the southern bird dog, as you shall see from this study of the beast.

Southerners are, as many outsiders suspect, stubborn, opinionated, backward-looking, anachronistic. We unabashedly admit to these markers and indeed consider their expression as complimentary. Modernity in none of its forms, including the introduction of new kinds of hunting dogs, is acceptable. As territory shrinks, we may have to eat crow and even let a Vizsla or Drahthaar into the county. But not yet! Not yet!

Misunderstandings occur when we fail to define the subject. Aaron Pass, in the initial issue of *Pointing Dog Journal* in 1993, contributed much to the paucity of literature that might serve to describe just what kind of canine meets a southerner's understanding of "bird dog." Aaron used to buy some stuff from me when he was editing a southern hunting magazine, and he now lives in Georgia. He is quite competent to draw a word picture, as he does in this paragraph: "The Dixie bird dog is a quail dog—and that's that. Across the length and breadth of the Southland, a 'bird dog' is born, bred, and genetically engineered to hunt, find, and point *Colinus virginianus*, the bobwhite quail."

In a chapter of my book *Sundown Covey* entitled "What's a Bird Dog?," I hope I contributed to the definition by beginning with the word "bird." From that chapter: "It never ceases to amaze me, however, that here in the South there could be any individual who, when I said I was going birdhunting, asks me 'what kind of bird?' I am on that sub-

ject, completely tunnel visioned. 'Bird' equals 'quail.' Only having established that exclusivity may we presume to define '*bird*' dog." Pass and I being in concurrence then, I need only add that to qualify as a bird dog, it must also have a tail, and be nearly white.

A footnote should explain that "quail" superceded "partridge," or more phonetically "pat 'ritch" or "poddige," on the tongues of southerners sometime in the twenties or thirties. Archibald Rutledge called it a "Yankee invasion." Havilah Babcock wrote of quail in *Tales of Quail and Such*. Old men spoke of partridges when I was growing up in the post-World War I era. There was no misidentification— grouse simply were unknown except in the mountains, so oldsters were talking about the small brown bomber that coveys up for the convenience of pointing dogs and smoothbore gunners. Or did behave that way in Babcock's time. Their scarcity now is a tragedy.

With the relatively rare exception of a Brittany here and there, the Dixie bird dog is always what is registered with the *American Field* as Pointer or Setter, or their unregistered offspring. In literature they are English Pointers and English Setters. Charles Fergus directs our attention to the misnomer, at least as to the Pointer, by people "not recognizing that the breed flowered here in North America where U.S. and Canadian hunters developed the Pointer into a dog that could reach out and handle the wide open spaces and large blocks of cover then prevalent on our continent." And, as you shall see, in both breeds the coats are almost always as near white as a breeder can develop. There are cogent reasons for this, and the coloration is sought by all the facets of bird-dog-dom—foot hunting, hunt-to-retrieve, open all-age.

Not so with the bench contestants, particularly with the Setters. Those gloriously beautiful animals, principally of American Kennel Club registry, are truly excluded from our definition. Davis Tuck's *The New Complete English Setter* is devoted almost exclusively to the show dogs, and the plethora of pictures of the ribboned dogs with Ch. preceding the name illustrates the differences in conformation and coat, as well as color, from the working bird dog in whatever category.

I talked by phone recently with Alfred King Sr., of Conway, Arkansas, who last year published *The Llewellin Setter*. The very existence of such a volume points out that, in this essay, we must recognize not only the types of activities in which working bird dogs engage but also the subdivisions within the breeds. This is more true of the Setters, there being historic bloodlines to be discussed. Pointers are more uniform, at least in appearance, and less has been written about their history.

In undertaking to write about these, my most favorite four-legged friends, I first inquired as to the existence of books or other literature that would help us better understand why these two breeds and no others have preempted the field here in the south Atlantic, Deep South, and Texas-Oklahoma territories. There is damned little set down on paper, for example, on the Pointer side except through *American Field* and William F. Brown's books (one written with Buckingham). You can run the list of field-trial champions, but that only says that Pointers and Setters are good up North or out West or in New England, or Canada. But go read Denny Argue's beautifully designed book, *Pointers and Setters*. Argue is English, and he still talks about dogs that "drop." He does relate the history of the Pointer in England, and the export of the breed to the States. The illustrations in that book will make you drool!

Mr. A.F. Hochwalt's little book, *Bird Dogs*, published in 1922, is a wellspring of information about specific Pointer breeding at the turn of the century and in the twenties, when Pointers superceded Setters in winning the big field-trial events. Nowhere have I been able to locate any litany on the short-haired smokeburner relating to southern heritage. But the affinity does exist!

Written wisdom being less than helpful, I took the liberty of inquiring from dog men across this ten-state territory their rationalization of the phenomenon: Why Pointers and Setters? Why will they not even *try* the exotics, the versatiles?

Some of their replies are set out as we progress through this monograph.

My own kennel over forty years has had its share of both Pointers and Setters. If I had to make a selection among those welcome boarders at my place, I'd have to note three Setters and one Pointer. Did I love one better than the others? Did one produce more birds? Any one easiest to train? No, all satisfied totally the elements of the bird-dog definition. But all had, in addition, that indefinable quality that sets both types apart from the rest of those that would aspire to be called bird dogs. It's that special significance that I'll try to explore in the balance of this report.

First, however, let's trace the history of the breeds, beginning with the Setter. For many of you readers, some of this is familiar territory. But both Tuck and King have real and documented information tracing the longhairs in Britain back to Spanish Spaniels and various outbreedings. Unquestionably, history indicates that these dogs were bred to "set," with the idea that, after locating game, they would lie or crouch so that a net could be thrown over dog and game. The slowness of gun loading—measuring the powder and shot, patching, ramrodding, and firing—had not given way to the breechloader, and since the purpose of hunting was more for meat than sport, the functional approach worked just fine. Later, as wing-shooting developed along with the revolution in firearms, erect pointing was bred into the practice. It was apparently at this stage that there came a division between the flushing and the pointing breeds. Argue notes that the need for a stand-up point came with American geography, where taller cover made droppers useless.

From time past, the rich and famous, and particularly the powerful—that is, the kings and knights and sheiks and others of the ruling class—had hunted with raptors. Early French tapestries depict falconry with the hunter usually mounted, a strange-looking long-haired low-built dog or dogs out in front, and a hooded falcon or other hawk jessed on the hunter's wrist. From what I can read about that sport, the dog would locate fur or feathers, hold until the bird (which learned to watch the dog) had wheeled into position, and then flush the partridge, quail, grouse, duck, or hare for the stoop. Even today, Steve Bodio waxes brilliantly literate in describing the thrills of combining hunting with dog and "long-wing."

But these are not our dogs. American English Setters trace principally from two British lines: the Laverack and the Llewellin. Obviously, this is overly simplistic. It is said that a Mister Edward Laverack, a breeder, trainer, and trader of hunting dogs in about 1875, learned of Setters in the kennels of the Earl of Carlisle that were descendants of French hunting dogs from the kennels of Louis VIII given to King James I of England half a century before. Alfred King researched the written reports of the day, including the *Classic Encyclopedia* of the 1880s, and even goes back to Laverack's own book, *The Setter*. From Carlisle the line found its way to a Reverend Harrison, from whom Laverack acquired the now-famous Old Moll and bred her back to her full brother, Ponto. These dogs were blue belton, that is, dark-speckled, but said by Laverack to be "the most perfect specimen of Setter I have ever seen." Their progeny, sold into America, became the progenitors of what I believe to be the show dogs of great beauty and the dogs of long heads and soulful eyes mostly hunted in the North for grouse and woodcock. Typical would be the Ryland and Old Hemlock lines. My own lack of experience with these, as distinguished from the Llewellin more prevalent in my part of the country, is going to prompt the Laverack-type owners to give me hell for some less than enthusiastic reporting. Who said, "It is better to keep one's mouth shut and be thought a fool than to open it and remove all doubt?"

As Mr. Laverack grew older, he became more set in his opinion that outcrosses destroyed his pure line. He did, however, dedicate his book to a younger Welshman, R.L. Purcell Llewellin, who had been breeding Irish and Gordons, but who was to make bird-dog history by combining the Duke, Rhoebe, and Laverack lines, leading to the ultimate Llewellin-type American hunting and field-trial Setter. The trend toward lighter color strengthened, and the tricolor became the standard. Gladstone is credited with being the original grandaddy of this special line, featuring a finer head and being a longer-legged dog, about which Mr. King rhapsodizes.

Llewellin had bought up all the Laveracks he could find. The Duke line was established through Sir F. Graham, and although some reported him a "trailer" rather than the preferred "winder," he was said to be remarkably successful in the field. I was puzzled to find that a strong contributor to the Llewellin we know today was a bitch named Rhoebe, an almost black, low-hung specimen not even remotely resembling our modern dog. Nevertheless, she threw strong field-trial winners. The King book, which is must-reading on the subject, quotes *The Dog Book*, by James Watson (1912), as saying, "At the American shows both sorts have appeared, and the Rhoebe blood has always beaten the Laverack." Hockwalt is quoted as saying that the mixture of Duke, Rhoebe, and Laverack bloodlines originated by Mr. Llewellin were "Llewellin Setters," no matter who bred them.

Of this breeding, dog brothers Dan and Dick and their sister Dora became important names in the line, particularly when the dogs were bred to the Laverack bitches. And Dora's offspring were said to be exceptional hunters. Out of these unions came the great Gladstone and his successors. *American Field* records show Count Gladstone IV as winner of the first national championship in this country, in 1896. During the first seventeen runnings of the National, from 1896 through 1915, Setters won fifteen times. I noted especially, however, that Sport's Peerless Pride, out of North Carolina, did win in 1939, and this was personally important, because my kennel boasted those bloodlines from the pharmacist Dr. Bobbitt of Winston-Salem. And Eugene M was champion in 1911, with Eugene's Ghost a Field Trial hall-of-famer, both ancestors of my Spook.

Outside Argue and Hochwalt, I simply have not found enough historical reference about the Pointer to compare with the meticulous record of the breeding of the Setter. Almost every reference presupposes that there is both English Bulldog and English Foxhound, plus some of the Spanish Spaniel, in what we now identify as Pointer. It is certainly true that English, that is, American, Pointers tend to look alike, although of course you think you can spot the Elhew head anywhere. But look at the wonderful pictures in Mr. Brown's book, and the magnificent Pointers that took control of field trials bear a startling resemblance to one another. They have been bred to be high in front and rear, to avoid sickle tail, to be broad of chest and strong in hindquarters, and almost every winner pictured is essentially all white or sparingly marked, mostly on the head, with black, tan, lemon, or liver. These field-trial specialists are of course separated in function from the walking hunter's pride. In this context, the speed, go, and intensity are diluted. Many writers say that foot-hunting dogs are simply those culled from the list of contenders for the National. But I know a number of breeders who work solely to produce the kind of dog I've described as a southern bird dog. This is not to say that we expect, nor will we tolerate, a dog that hangs underfoot. Indeed, our quarrel with the versatiles is our perception that the imports fail to range when necessary. The very soul of the characteristics we demand is the ability to adapt. And this is where Pointers and Setters so excel. They both, more than any other breed, adapt to our variable landscape—from swamp to hundred-acre bean field, from rough briars to the Colonel's pea patch.

· 13 ·
We Poll the Experts

Charles Fergus says that Pointers took over because they were faster than Setters, found more birds, matured more quickly, and were better able to "accept strict, even harsh discipline." His conclusion that Pointers excel in the game coverts will raise explosive denials from the Setter crowd.

Tuck says of the Setter, "It has retained its popularity since its introduction to the United States primarily because of its usefulness, beauty, lovable disposition, loyalty and devotion." He goes on to say, I'm pleased to note, that the "hunting ability of the English Setter is not soiled but enhanced by making it a family pet."

Jeff Griffin, in his *Hunting Dogs of America*, when writing about pointing dogs generally is dogmatic (no pun intended) that all pointing dogs should be steady to wing and shot, a hot topic for discussion among foot hunters, who are likely to disagree. He also attempts to make a case for the universal acceptance of the imports. His arguments to my mind are simply not persuasive. A review of the reports of 1993 South Carolina NBHA trials, with several hundred entries, disclosed only one outside the Pointer and Setter breeds. Whether from prejudice, ignorance, or stubbornness, these two are uniquely accepted in my area.

Let's inquire, then, of people who now or in the past have quail-hunted throughout the South. Why, we ask, do dogs so enthusiastically supported elsewhere—that is, the

German Shorthairs, Vizslas, and so on—fail miserably in the geographical areas that are, or were at one time, the veritable home base of the bobwhite? Surely it is not just prejudice or pride of territory. I will guarantee that of the guys contributing to this chapter, any one would pledge his grandmother for the best-producing bird dog available—not just from up North, but from anywhere in the world. If a Rhodesian Ridgeback could outhunt, outpoint, and outretrieve the Pointers and Setters on our terrain, some of these fellows would put a second mortgage on the homestead to finance the acquisition.

Stan Meares, of Hickory, North Carolina, is a retired banker who brings to the dog breeding now dominating his time and efforts the exhaustive study that led him to exploit the Flatwood Hank line. He says, "In all honesty, a part of my preference [for Pointers and Setters] is pure tradition. I have owned and attempted to train Pointers and Setters for many years. During that time I have also owned and trained members of the versatile breeds." Meares quotes longtime dog trainer Paul Long, who in April of 1994 was named a Patron of the National Bird Dog Foundation: "In the South, Southwest, and Western Canada, dogs have been developed to run the edges and cast out to likely objectives. Differences in topography and agricultural methods dictate the needs of gunners in a particular region, and dogs of the region have been bred to meet those needs."

Meares continues: "In the region I hunt, it is not uncommon to hunt bean fields varying in size from one hundred to three hundred acres. Most of these fields are bordered by piney woods, thus a dog with range is required, and he must also handle and work close in wooded areas. I have heard of versatile breeds with these attributes—I just never have seen them."

Dr. Bob Payne, of Athens, Georgia, bird-hunts big time. An amateur, he really has the professional's knowledge of the birds and the dogs in low-country South Carolina, middle Georgia and northern Florida. He is a joy to hunt with because of these qualities and his ongoing sense of humor. But he is dead serious when he says, "I hunt in mixed territory, frequently in fields bordered by swamp or pines. Only white dogs with high tail on point can be seen by hunters under these circumstances." Bob holds his kennels to Thor lines from Alabama, or the old Rambling Rebel ancestry.

Wayne Dye of Midville, Georgia, is, along with others of his clan, widely known in the hunting fraternity of the area. Laconically, he says, "I don't give a damn, so long as they find birds and I can see 'em." But when last I hunted with him, he was true to tradition—Pointers and English or Llewellin Setters. He hunts from a big diesel pickup; his dogs, ranging out front, swing left on one toot, right on two toots, and return for relief on a long blast. His Eagle, now aged, is an exception to the color rule—a dark blue belton. Incidentally, Eagle doubles as Labrador in that he is a duck retriever of remarkable reputation.

Herbert Jenkins, of Aulander, North Carolina, easterly and close to the Virginia line, is a veteran of six decades of persistent seeking after *Colinus*. He may have during that time owned and personally hunted over as many dogs as anyone in the country. Some were good, some bad, and a few very, very good. But all were either Pointer or Setter. "The type of dog I am most familiar with is for walking hunters with either a mixture of open and thick territory—or all thick. These dogs must have shorter range [than field-trialers], especially in the thick, so that the hunter always knows where his dog is, or else the hunt becomes the hunt for the dog. While they come in many colors, the predominant color is always white. There is a very practical reason for this—visibility during the hunt. They don't have their tails docked. Many times bird hunters located dogs on point by seeing that white tail sticking up out of whatever thick cover the dog may be in."

And finally, Alfred King favored me with a special note that adds an ingredient to the choice: "The Llewellin cannot be beat; they are the same dogs that were on calendar prints in the 1920s to 1950s: the old dog with litter of pups on the hearth. These pups truly learn everything they need to know by socializing with you. Through housebreaking they learn what they can and cannot do; playing, they learn to retrieve, sit, stay, etc. They point instinctively even at a sock tied to a shoestring. In other words, everything that needs to be done can be done with pleasure."

My own coda to this symphony: Add the words "intelligence" and "affection"! Both Pointers and Setters learn quickly and both have a "smart" eye. Though some find the Pointer cold and hard, no dog could have been more loving than my Kate. Except Polly. Except Pat. Except Spook. Without love, you can run birds up with a Jeep, catch 'em in a net, shoot 'em on the ground.

In summary, then, if you live and hunt quailbirds south of the Mason-Dixon, you will want an intelligent *bird* dog that is adaptable to big fields and thick swamps; that is findable because of white color and high tail; that is inherently teachable and biddable; that will find, point, back, and retrieve; and that returns your respect and love—that means a Pointer or an English or Llewellin Setter. Like Spook. Nothing else can touch 'em.

· 14 ·

*I*nvestments

Note: This chapter first appeared as "Playing the Percentages" in *Covey Rises and Other Pleasures*.

Charlotte
Tuesday

Dear Herb,

Everything I read these days talks about a recession, and I got to takin' a look at my assets to see what kind of return I was gettin'. Figured I must be doin' better 'n most anybody when I considered everything.

Now just take my investment in birdhuntin'. I've put in about fifty sessions out of my threescore allotted years, and hope I've got some more stored away for the future. And it has paid off a sort of cumulated preferred dividend—each year I add to all the others the memories of what we lawyers call "the next preceding season." If you look at it that way, I've got a sizeable chunk of capital and it's compoundin' interest like crazy. And the beauty of it is, I don't ever spend it. Share it, but don't spend it.

For example, it's almost opening day and I'm sittin' here like some miser countin' his millions, and just reviewin' last season alone, I feel rich. Or better, take one Saturday, and see what it produced.

Bob White is a gentleman and doesn't get up early, so it's eight o'clock on a February morning. The boys and I have picked up the dogs, stopped at the Waxhaw Grill twenty miles down the road for grits and eggs and two cups of coffee. The truck has slid into the ruts of an old loggin' road, under a cedar and sorta out of sight of the next birdhunter comin' by. No need to advertise the woods covey halfway between the pickup and the bean field.

*Old Spook and Polly Who? (that's her registered name)
have busted hell for leather straight for the bicolor patch, and Pete's
Buck is ranging off to the right. It's forty degrees and the hoarfrost
is standing in the wagon tracks as stiff and gray as my whiskers. A
fox has rousted the woods birds, and they're sure to have flown to
the soybeans, and anyway, that's the breakfast table for at least two
other coveys, regularly.*

So *we come out of the pines and hit a strip of broomstraw and three dogs are marbleized out front. And for the next five minutes you find yourself projected into some slow-motion sequence, like in a picture show. You know the feelin'. Sort of a sense of unreality—as though you're standin' off watchin' yourself go through the ritual. Not déjà vu. It's happening now. But strangely detached.*

You take the center, and step up toward the point. On your left, peripheral vision tells you your big old bearded boy (you can't realize he's old enough for law school) has swung his 16 pump to ready. Right side, and there's a six-foot son-in-law you actually like, growling an unmentionable as a random briar bush grabs his ear. Your little 20 gauge comes up so smoothly you are never conscious that you've flicked the safety as the first bird flutters. And the old familiar never-expected, never-forgotten whrrr-r of the covey rise. The boys are blacked out as you follow a straightaway cock bird, and there's an explosion of feathers, but you're too greedy on the double. Suddenly the scene is frozen for you. A mental camera clicks with Spook mouthin' his retrieve and Polly chasin' a cripple through the blackberry bushes, and Buck tenderly handin' Pete one of his two kills. And the whole thing is etched on your memory like one of the frames in a slide projector, full-color: dark green loblollies, backing golden straw field, brown blobs of hunters, white, white setters, sky now dolomite blue, and cotton tufts of cloud just touched with slanting sunshine.

The day goes on and old Spook is tired. He's had his full, unbelievable fourteen years of single-minded, unblemished dedication. Old dog, old friend. The truck's a while away. And when he stops and sags, the Boy hands you his gun and swings the grand old man onto his broad young shoulders and helps repay the hours when dog broke boy. You're touched at the mutual affection, and love for them both is a very real thing.

But what a day! Seven, by golly, seven coveys found, pointed, and shot over. A respectable number of quail snuggled in each huntin' vest, and plenty left for seed.

And what a payoff. If you figure 624 available bird-huntin' hours to the season, here on this short Saturday you've only committed six. That means you've put in, today, only $^1/_{106}$ of your investible capital. You can turn your memory-money over, like your inventory, at least once a month for the rest of the year, so I conclude that's a nine hundred percent profit. Try turning that through your minicomputer. And tell me any stock, Big Board or Amex, that can touch it.

Birdhuntin', boy. What an investment!

Sincerely,

David

· 15 ·

Day of Infamy

---

*T*he upstairs rooms where the visiting hunters sleep were chilly at wake-up time. It was late December, between Christmas and New Year. I shivered as I threw off the covers and stepped to the window. What would be the mood of the day?

The open fields where summer crops had grown stretched westward, the first rays of winter sun climbing tentatively behind me. The visage of my world, at least the part of it I could see, had overnight sprouted a grizzled beard of hoarfrost. The new light, now rising above the ridgepole, struck millions of diamonds, bejeweling the landscape all the way to the edge of the pine woods. Pippa was passing, so I tipped my imaginary cap to this *éminence gris*. Good morning, World, I thought. It can't get any better than this! Later in the day it got worse, as you shall see.

But it was my world. I was home, in the heart of the ancestral seat of my mother's family, and I'm talking deep southern roots. I was at Herbert and Skippy's house, transported 250 miles east of my city of residence for my annual bird hunt, and it was to be special. I had brought young Spook, high-blooded Setter, to show him off to the master.

The master, of course, and this was in the sixties, was and is now cousin Herbert Jenkins, bird hunter par excellence for five decades. Herbert is not so tall as I, probably five feet seven inches, with blocky build, a cap of whitening hair, an outdoorsman's coloring, and an indefatigable stride. He neither smokes nor drinks, nor, however, does he proselytize his friends. By the time I got downstairs he was in briarbritches, but still in slippers. "Well, good mornin'," he said. "You know, I'm lookin' forward to seein' that Spookdog you wrote about." I should have been warned that the youngster was in for a day under a very critical eye. Or rather that I, his boss, would have to answer for any indiscretion.

Alice Jenkins has been called "Skippy" so long I sometimes find it hard to remember her real name. She has fed and housed more bird hunters over the past fifty years than any professional hunting lodge. "Hello," she greeted me. "I'll have breakfast in a little while. How's Maxine? And the kids?" She was stirring around in her wrapper, hair not yet dressed for the day, but absolutely mistress of her kitchen. "Thanks for the Christmas poetry. And you might want to read a little something I put on paper." She and I share some admiration for the muse, although I suspect "How do I love thee" might yet be her favorite in all literature. She is a very special person.

Herbert was reading the *News and Observer* ("Covers East Carolina Like the Dew"). He seemed in no rush to get on with my goals for the day. "Bob White isn't going anywhere," he observed. "The little gentleman will wait for us. We'll get out of here about ten. I need to talk to a couple of tobacco farmers about our warehouse sale before I take off. Then we'll maybe pick up a couple of coveys before lunch, eat at Slade's store, and have all afternoon to see whether you really brought a bird dog, or just sumpin' pretty."

He quietly asked a blessing at table, reached for a glass of orange juice, and proceeded to load scrambled eggs and a slice of "old bacon" ham onto the plate. The latter is smokehouse-cured for a minimum of two years and, like Italian prosciutto, can be eaten without cooking. It is a creation of some culinary genius in heaven, and blends with eggs as naturally as pancakes do with syrup. It is not to be confused with store-bought "country ham," which is pumped with curing fluid at some hog factory. You cannot buy such a delicacy. It is simply kept for company, and special company at that. So you can see where I stand in this household.

Herbert's kennels are fifty yards back of the house. The in-town lot runs another two hundred yards to the "canal," a drainage ditch cut by mule and drag-pan a hundred years ago to take away wastewater from the streets of the little town of Aulander. The back side of the property is frequently the site for deer, sometimes in groups of several. This is, of course, a modern phenomenon. Bertie County for the past quarter-century has had a population explosion of the creatures that, in my boyhood, were not to be seen outside the swamps. We went out the back door to the parked pickup, opened the double dog box, and went to select the day's participants.

The kennel runs exit from a concrete-block house about fifty feet long that serves for feed and bedding storage and gives access to the indoor, two-level, sleeping quarters. Thus bedding can be changed, sick dogs doctored, bitches' quarters turned to whelping pens all from inside. And it's very cozy, especially when chores have to be done in cold weather. Each outside run is about six by fifteen feet, has a smooth concrete base for easy washing, and a nipple self-serving watering system except in freezing weather. A pressure hose cleans floors daily, and a drain and septic tank make for a healthy environment. Nothing is foolproof, and I have been on hand when a stop-up created a problem just in time to interfere with going hunting. But that goes with keeping dogs.

At two dogs to the run, the setup can accommodate fourteen bird dogs, but seldom holds more than ten unless holding for visitors. Spook seemed perfectly happy in his guest quarters, and was bubbling to go. I had brought only Spook, properly relying on Herbert to have a sufficiency of quail-finders, most of which would be "broke" in a bird-hunting sense. In the last fifty years, Herbert has never had a short-tailed dog of his own in those kennels. Last year, however, somebody did give him a Brittany puppy he couldn't graciously refuse.

I could hardly wait to get going. Aside from the sheer pleasure of quailhunting with Herbert, I was anxious to show him what a genius of a young dog I had come up with. Just short of twelve months, Spook at home was well within my definition of *broke*. He was performing almost flawlessly either when hunted alone or in company. He was far and away the better dog than Frank, the Pointer I'd dispensed with a year before. Even some of my hunting buddies, notorious for their jealousy about dogs, said nice things about him. This day he was put down with a couple of strange dogs, but it didn't phase him.

By now the sun was halfway to noon, and as we worked along a little creek bottom, a fallow field upslope flashed what must have been a million cobwebs lacing each dried weed. None was larger than a man's hand, and all were backlit by the sun through melted frost in brilliant splendor.

It was as though Nature had sewn sequins on a gossamer gown and dressed herself for a ball. I can still remember the loveliness, and thinking how impermanent is beauty.

I think we were on lands owned by a kinsman, probably Bill Marsh or his wife, Martha, but Herbert has lots of hunting rights. He maintains them by exercising supreme care of the land. Never does he track through a muddy farm road. He parks and walks. Nor does he countenance taking a chance with firing another's woodlands. If you smoke, be careful, or switch to smokeless.

Happily I watched Spook work the edges of a bean field, turning on my whistle and finally pointing in a briared corner. We killed a couple. Next, one of Herbert's dogs located, Spook backed, and on the gun Herbert's little Randy flashed in and retrieved ahead of the bigger guys. Things were going extremely well. We worked out through a right-of-way, one of those with steel giants striding along the center, feet covered by waving broomstraw. Then through a country churchyard, and we were in sight of Slade's Signboard Schoolhouse Store. The alliteration slithered sibilantly. (Hey! How's that?)

"Let's try that little five-acre field across from the store, and then we'll eat," said my hunting partner. To this point he had been singularly noncritical—of the visiting Setter.

Because lunch was to be anticlimactic after the five-acre field, you ought to, at this point, meet Washington Slade. An old abandoned frame schoolhouse served as site for his country store emporium. There this universally respected and well-liked black man plied his trade as merchant, garageman, cook, and operator of the neighborhood pool hall. His custom was both black and white, and on cold winter days his roaring barrel stove warmed all alike, the patrons standing hip-to-hip to absorb the radiant heat. It was, in this once-prejudiced neighborhood, a validation of Harry Golden's observation that there was no discrimination so long as everybody stood up.

At Slade's place, the hoop cheese was always ripest, the Pepsis always coldest, the sausage biscuits hottest. Once in a while Mrs. Slade would bring over from their house across the paved road some portion of rabbit or possum, and favored guests would be entitled to a gustatory delight. But most important, this couple, in an unbelievable atmosphere of division in some parts of the South, managed to send all— I believe seven—of their children to college. A beautiful daughter, the last of the youngsters I remember, had just graduated from Elizabeth City Community College.

The little field, Herbert pointed out, should be worked from the roadside back to the tree line. "Put Spook on your right, and I'll take the other dogs to this side, and maybe we'll have some luck."

Have luck? Bad luck, that is! Spook had no sooner crossed the road shoulder than he made game. I moved up and a single flushed. I fired wildly. Thus encouraged, my paragon of a bird dog began a race to see if he could put up every quail in a scattered fifteen-bird covey. I screamed. I whistled. I shouted. To no avail. Herbert looked sick at this missed opportunity. I could have cried with embarrassment. I didn't eat much lunch at Slade's.

"Well, you said he could find birds," Herbert said

laconically. Normally a kind and gentle man, he has never let me forget this incident. Like an earlier day in December, this went down as a "day that will live in infamy."

/

· 16 ·
The Dogs

Spook, of course, was not the only bird dog in the Henderson kennels. Not being a breeding operation as such, we never found it necessary to give a name to the institution. But the location of the dog pens changed from time to time as the family moved through three different houses. We always tried to have dog quarters adjacent to home, rather than parked out at some outlying farm, because I firmly believe in the "proximity approach." That is, the closer you are to your dogs every day, the better producers they will be on hunt days. Maybe that's ill stated. Perhaps I should say the more biddable the dog will be when out of the wire. Never, however, in the forty-year span I'm covering, have I had facilities to accommodate active bird dogs inside the house. The Labradors, yes, but Pointers and Setters—not in Maxine's domain.

I've mentioned my first Pointer, Frank, and his wayward ways. Noteworthy among the many guests over the next four decades would be Mack, Snoopy, Kate, and Pat.

Mack was a peer of Spook's. I recall that, as I tried him out, a prospective buy from a deputy sheriff, I had knocked down a cock bird inside a thick hedgerow on land belonging at the time to Billy Graham, whose parents were neighbors of ours. I sent Mack into the thicket and was vocally berating him for not showing some class retrieving when the sheriff quietly said, "Look behind you, David." Sure enough, Mack was sitting directly behind me, and he carefully laid the bird to hand.

Purists don't care for pointing dogs to "go around." Some think this to be blinking, or evidence of gun-shyness or bird-shyness. Only in reading the history of the pointing dogs and their evolution do you find that this is an inherited sense of "smarts," allowing a net hunter to cast over an otherwise running covey. Mack was a master of the cutoff, and his quick retrieves belied any psychoses about contact.

I had with him a frightening experience when hunting in the Waxhaw Creek area, alone with only Mack and Spook. Mack was unaccountably lost, a rare event for a close-working dog. Spook was ranging, and I hied him forward, hoping to find Mack on point. It was a while before they showed up, Spook seeming to lead the other dog, who had a great, gaping hole in his flank, with only a membrane holding in his guts. In retrospect, he probably tore it on a barbwire. Too far from the truck to carry his fifty pounds, I walked slowly. Then the gameness of old Mack showed through. Passing behind an old garden site, Mack turned, walked ten steps, and pointed. The big covey blew out without this astonished hunter's nicking a feather.

Snoopy was a short-legged Setter bought for, I think, a hundred dollars from a farmer in the north of the county. She was a fine singles dog, usually yielding first point to some more aggressive dog. But, boy, would she *back*!

I never knew her to break another's point. Again we must look to the history of Setters, because Snoopy carried over the genes that had prompted dogs to drop, that is, go flat, on point. Netters demanded that dogs be trained to drop to facilitate the cast. She was, however, the only dog I ever had that had epilepsy. In the midst of a hunt, and especially in game, she would suddenly fall over, apparently dying. In five minutes, the fit would have passed and she would be on her merry way. This was not the old-fashioned "running fit" caused by worms and now scarcely ever seen. Nor was it a blood sugar deficiency, because candy in the field was not a preventative.

Kate was one of the few Pointers. Emotionally, I find it hard to write about her. She would have nothing to do with women, even those who love pets. In bird-finding and other hunting skills, she was incomparable. In affection, she was surpassed only by my Polly.

Pat was a true blue belton tricolor Llewellin. She had all the bloodlines and all the skills. A fabulous retriever, especially on a long-sailing wing-tipped bird, she would delight you with the surprise bird-to-hand returned from some distant briarpatch. Mammary gland problems, which so frequently cost us our favorite bitches, hit Pat hard. Only the splendid efforts of veterinarians at the Matthews Clinic saved her for us for a few extra years. A complete radical stripped her, but she continued to hunt in exemplary fashion. Well, she did begin to self-hunt, which we blamed on the scarcity of game. But when on point, an earthquake would not call her off. We'd come up on her, deep in some swamp cover, locked in like a picture from *Pointing Dog Journal*. D.L. and I miss her badly.

Rebel's Polly Who? was so special, and her pairing with Spook so remarkable, that I've saved her for another chapter.

· 17 ·
The Guns

I have never been mechanically inclined, and I know little, nor do I care greatly about, the intricacies of the manufacture of shotguns, nor of the ballistics so cleverly written about by Bodio, McIntosh, and Boothroyd. I read their books in hope of someday achieving a bit of knowledge that will let me participate in conversations around a lodge fire when the guys bring out their vintage Parkers, A.H. Foxes, Elsies, and perhaps Purdeys. All I have to offer, even at this late date of association, is my love of guns as works of art and mechanics, and a feel for fit when I pick up a strange weapon in a gun store.

Hanging on the wall of the den of my son D.L., there are two smoothbores passed down in the family from my father's father, a couple of locally made hunting arms with ramrods still attached. These are not fine, but they do reflect the hunting tradition that runs six measurable generations from Ezekiel Henderson down to my grandson, Patrick. There are also on the fireplace a couple of breechloaders, one with nipples, and the Johannsen with its huge rabbit ears.

I started D.L. off with a Harrington Richardson single-barrel 20 gauge as a learner on dove shoots. Then one of the Savage-Fox factory-made doubles in the fifties. He quickly learned that the stock was malformed, the grip too ponderous, and the gun forward-heavy, and without even asking, he traded it somewhere for a 16 gauge Ithaca pump. He was surprisingly deadly with this model, which had, as

you may recall, the turned forepiece. When it was stolen, along with an Ithaca 12 (in fancy sheepskin case), he replaced it with the more modern Ithaca pump, but this time with the modified splinter fore-end. Only lately come by is his current gun of choice. It is a classic 16 gauge Parker side-by-side, obtained from an impecunious friend who left it for collateral for a loan, and who then ultimately released it. It had belonged to his father, and when he at some later date brought along the original published piece from the purchase box, I almost cried that this youngster had had to give up part of his heritage. The leg-o'-mutton leather case that came with the gun had been badly abused.

On my own den walls hang two relics of World War II, souvenirs shipped back from an arms dump at the Salzburg airport, where they had been unceremoniously thrown on a pile of weaponry seized from Bavarian households. Many of the items were antiques, handmade by local German gun makers. Others were clearly of museum quality. All were destined, I suppose, for the bulldozer, except for those rescued by GIs. With a bit of imagination, they could be shipped back to the States at government expense. I mention them here because they are hunters' artwork, beautifully made with skilled and loving hands for use in the Bavarian Alps. One of mine is unique in that it was designed to be a target rifle in some castle basement range. It has a firing pin that runs to within ten inches of the end of the barrel and fires a .17 cartridge loaded from underneath. The dollar value is, I suppose, substantial; a similar piece has a place in a current Sotheby auction catalogue.

My own small gun collection, if that's what one would call it, is limited to functional stuff that has relatively little monetary value. I do not keep it where thieves and robbers can get at it, except for the little Remington 20 gauge that has followed me to the bird fields these last twenty years. Gun writers uniformly regale us with data on the "Best Guns." The best for me are those smoothbores that let me put a quail on the ground at twenty yards, and just maybe a second at thirty-five. Through the years, the best of those has been a 12 gauge Franchi O/U bored skeet one and skeet two.

I have an idea that Spook was glad to see the boss get something he could bust a covey with, but I found the trigger guard banging my middle finger on every shot and foolishly traded instead of restocking. I never could shoot the Winchester Model 12, having had no boyhood practice on pumps. A 20 gauge Franchi O/U has gone to a grandson. The big Belgian Browning A5 is now simply too heavy to haul around. Besides, I hate trying to remember how to change the O-rings when switching from high brass to low as we go from geese to doves. A fine old Ithaca in 12 gauge open/open is the ultimate bird gun for the side-by-side fellow, so that is in the hands of D.L. There's a double .410 in my bedroom corner loaded with #5s in case an intruder—oh, that's not really likely. Or is it?

· 18 ·

A Few of the Guys

A recipe for birdhunting requires four ingredients. They are birds, dogs, guns, and guys. I have not said much about the bobwhite quail except to indicate that *Colinus virginianus* is the be-all and end-all of what we in the South mean when we say "bird." I shall not abuse the precept, electing to honor each hunter's choice of game—each "king of gamebirds," up to the wild turkey, *Meleagris gallopavo silvestris,* a substantially larger member of the gallinaceous order, sharing, I think, the characteristic of having three toes forward and one back. That said, and having shown off my bit of Latin, I'll move on.

Elsewhere are chapters on dogs and guns. Herewith a portion of profiles. Cousin Herbert has listed maybe a hundred hunters with whom he has shared time in the fields. I have hunted with not so many. Indeed, I may have been the more fortunate, because for the fewer number of days I was privileged to hunt, I hunted more often with the same few.

I am very jealous of that limited time. I try never to carry shotguns with people I would not want to spend other time with. Ergo, my hunting companions of major note were Beachum, Cousin Herbert, and my son, D.L. Bluntly, if any of them be available, I don't need excess baggage. It is just that most Saturdays I knew Beachum and I would be working Waxhaw Creek, and after the Judge, D.L. and I took every opportunity to work together, a much-appreciated father-son team.

Of course, there were other notable fellows it was fun to be with and whose prowess I admired. One was Bob Sanders, ten years my junior, who moved in next door while Spook was young. Bob was already a hard hunter keeping a substantial kennel of Pointers and Setters either at Waxhaw with Collins or with a trainer named J. Von Robinson. Jayvon was named (which is Southern for "has a reputation") as an overly tough trainer, too handy with a flushing whip. I once placed with him a fine-looking pup, one of Spook's as a matter of fact. He said, "I'll break him in thirty days, or no pay." I found him as good as his word. The pup never wanted to come in to hunt close, and I was charged no fee—not even board—and the dog showed no signs of abuse, either. So Mr. Robinson still stands high in my estimation. He and Bob hunted together a long time. Sanders even had a special "dogotel" built to fit on his pickup. It held six dogs on each side, but somebody had to lift the passengers into the top bunks. There was a time when he and I either hunted together or crossed paths somewhere in the area over quite a spell. Always the soul of southern courtesy, he was a pleasure to have as a neighbor and hunting partner.

Bill Callum worked for a motor line, had time, and actually was expected to take customers hunting. That he also took me, and many times only me, was not recorded on the company's time sheets. He will not be offended too much when I relate that he was not easy to get along with, was opinionated, and had to change territories often. He will not be offended, because in the same breath I must say that he was, and may yet be, a damned good birdhunter, a fine shot, and as hard a walker as you are likely to find. He was indefatigable in seeking out hunting areas, sometimes a hundred or so miles away, and he never forgot to take a present for the landowner or his family. But he was hard on hunting partners. "Dave," he would often, but erroneously comment, "you always shoot better when you're with me." That was unsolicited canard.

It was through Bill that I first ventured into Indian country, the County of Robeson, being east of home and populated heavily with Lumbee Indians. No white strangers fared happily there. Cut tires were expected; cut ribs a possibility. Callum, however, had traded there for bird dogs, and had developed guide relationships. For five dollars, a local would accompany two hunters all day, usually but not always managing to avoid conflict with landowners. Once, a Chavis (or a Hunt or Oxendine or Locklear, the most common local names), however, stayed in the car claiming a sore knee, but he pointed us around a patch of woodland where we found an operating moonshine still. For an outlander who might be a "Revenoor," to even be in the neighborhood of such an operation will get you killed, and we were lucky the operator had gone home for lunch or something. "Hell," said Bill, "you damned near got us shot!" No five dollars for that guide!

Callum rightly predicted an end to our regular hunts. "You've gone and spoiled it," he said. "Got your own dog. Now you'll be wanting to have him on the ground all the time, and I'll want mine hunting—and it just won't work." We tried it a few times, but he thought me a bit amateurish, and I thought him overly critical, so gradually we drifted in different directions. But there are still some Callum stories to be told here.

John Collins and his wife, Clyde (yep, Clyde), owned fifty or so acres just out of the little town of Waxhaw, close onto the North Carolina–South Carolina line. John was a professional "trader," with all that implies. Of course, he farmed a bit, and boarded hunting dogs, and broke colts, but one suspected that he made his real living with his wits in buying and selling horses and mules. "Dave," he'd say. "You see that bay colt? Well, he's the nearest thing to Big Red [or some other big name] that you ever will see." Now the youngster possibly had no drop of racehorse blood, but with John it was caveat emptor. Once, birdhunting in South Carolina, I met a landowner who asked me if I knew a fellow named Collins from Waxhaw. I hedged the conversation until I learned the reason for the inquiry. "That Collins, one day, traded my daddy a mule. Daddy had always said you could tell a good mule by the way its ears pricked. This one looked especially alert. Daddy thought he'd skunked Collins when he talked him out of the halter, free. When he got home and took off the halter, underneath and holding up the ears he found two big rubber bands." The birdhunters listening in *wha-whaed* in laughter.

I wrote the obituary for John in the county paper and told that story. The family was pleased as punch. Clyde said, "You really knew John." He was a fine horseman, and at seventy-five rode like a centaur. It was at John's that Beachum kept his dogs, including the redoubtable Pat. Almost every Saturday, we'd pick up the dogs there and hunt the Massey and Heath properties nearby. After the hunt we'd go inside, where Clyde would have a slice of fruit cake, a glass of wine, or hot coffee for cold hunters. She'd fuss all the time about John's propensity for a touch of bourbon behind the barn, but she was a kind and gentle soul and loved every one of us unto the second generation.

This was the same John that, early in our acquaintance told me, with straight face, "There was this little ole Pointer bitch showed up at the fillin' station one fall. She followed Don Street off birdhuntin' one day and he come back amazed at how good she was. After that we all hunted her, and she hunted for everybody, then just disappeared. Night of that big blizzard in 1933. Found her skeleton in June. Her skeleton and the skeleton of eight quails in front of her nose. Froze to death on point." At least two editors I know have reprinted that story (and presumably paid for it) in the past twenty years. It has made the rounds in every quail state in the Union. But John first told it to me.

Doctor Earle Spaugh was another in the coterie that hunted together in the sixties and seventies. He was suffering postpolio syndrome, a fact noted here because, in spite of limited use of his left hand and left leg, he never quit hunting and fishing with a remarkable zest. His two white Setters, along with Spook and my Mack dog, made a formidable threat to the quail population over two states. I remember one of his Setters retrieving from *inside* a hollow tree, where the whole dog had disappeared. And recently, he (at the time bedridden) and I recalled walking back to the truck after sunset with all four tired dogs on the ground, when all pointed or backed on a roosting roadside covey. Illegally, of course, I automatically fired, and the dogs brought in two birds out of the blackness. Dr. Spaugh died in early 1995.

I possibly have not said enough about D.L., my son, hunting buddy for twenty-five years, and best friend. Twice have I seen him make honest triples on a covey rise, a rare per-formance. Often I have seen him, like the rest of us, fail to cut a feather. Never have I seen him abuse a dog, kill over the limit, or fail to be a true sportsman. As I have said before, "He'll do to hunt with!"

· 19 ·

Backtrack

Note: This chapter first appeared as "Letter to my Cousin" in *Sundown Covey*.

Charlotte
Sunday Night

Dear Herbert:

It's about that time again. Persimmons are unaccountably ripe and sweet. My resident barn owls brought off a hatch in the spring, and the young ones are travel-talking about dusk. There's a flush of fall at daybreak, and I wrap my robe a little tighter when I send the Lab out to the street for the paper. Blackgum has crimsoned up in the hardwood stands and put the lie to the eighty-degree temperature in the dove fields. And so to more important seasons.

I was down at Briarpatch this afternoon and marked in the dust where a covey had meandered across the logging road. The quail tracks put me in mind of the time you and Jackie and I were hunting over beyond Ahoskie. My Spook dog was in his prime, and I always brought him along because he seemed to like hunting your eastern bays and bogs.

We had stopped the truck at the back side of a field where the farm road went through a sort of neck with a little ditch and woods coming up on either side. And, sure 'nuf, there in the sand were those telltale marks, three toes to the left, heel to the right—maybe a dozen sets. So we waved the dogs left through a section of soybeans, expecting a lock-up any minute, and certainly at the edge of the woods. Nuthin' doin'! All those grand dogs on the ground and no birds. Five broke smokeburners—no, Spook was missing, wouldn't come in on the whistle, and didn't answer a holler. I started looking hard, and having more faith in the old man than did you and Jackie, I went back across the road to the tracks that showed any birdhunter where the quail came from.

By golly, there he was—frozen in a honeysuckle thicket. The flag he inherited from Eugene's Ghost flew bravely, and he had that glazed look he got in his eye when there are quail tails up his nose. He'd found them all right. Y'see, Spook had learned in his trips down east just how smart your local birds were. They'd been in the beans when they heard your truck coming. So they walked backward *across the road, hoping to throw the dogs off. They just hadn't counted on the bird sense of the visiting veteran, Spook. Legends, Cousin, legends!*

All the best,

David

· 20 ·

Père et Fils

How many things we've shared these thirty years:

The shattered diamonds of a waterfall,
The soft sweet scent of hickory campfire smoke,
The lift of spirit at a bobwhite's call,
The antics of that puppy that we broke.

The smell of marsh, and whistling wings at dawn.
Both hearts to stutter at a covey flush,
The big king salmon hen released to spawn,
A mocker's song against the evening hush.

Your own first hunt, and how I wished you well,
The Lynches River float, and that big coon,
The lunker bass we caught, the lies we'd tell,
The lost and lonely goose against the moon.

Now your new boy must also learn to care,
We owe that duty to him and his peers,
The outdoor sights and sounds they need to share,
As we did in those passing happy years.

No lad has ever come here fully "broke,"
So Grandpére now will undertake that chore,
And hope that by some magic master-stroke,
I'll make a kid into a MAN—once more.

· 21 ·
Another Day

It's hard to remember all the exceptional hunting days Spook and I had together. Even in the seventies I was complaining about the loss of the bird population. Here's another day I wrote about to my birdhunting Cousin Herbert.

December 15, 1970

Dear Herbert:

Between us there lies, practically dormant, three-quarters of a century of birdhunting, now reduced by the vagaries of time to rarer forays to the sometimes haunts of His Honor, Robert. I say "sometimes," because neither he nor his kith or kin frequent the edge lines and hedgerows of the past. A conclusion is patent. There are no edges nor hedgerows left after thirty-foot gang plows and extended-arm ditchers have denuded the land and all of the habitat in the name of profit.

I see our old hunting buddies who taught us about hunting techniques now walking on arthritic knees or with aching backs, appearing to be in physical pain, but still trying to find some hope of success, if only in short bursts—maybe a couple miles an hour. Since we're past the halfway mark, I can see the future on the downhill side, and wonder if there'll be any game when we reach seventy-five, or if we'll be able to follow the dogs at all.

But to take you, however esoterically, from the confines of your dungeon den [H. was down in the back at the time], let me share with you last Saturday. There had been two days and two inches of rain, with the sun only biting a gap in the cloud cover about eleven. D.L. had already declared that "if it quits raining, I'm going somewhere this weekend." His call then at noon enticingly indicated that maybe Dad might, just might, want to try the wet brush, say from two o'clock to dark. He added that there was some promise of a short hunt at Granny's, an old friend of the family whose two hundred acres lie along a little creek that floods in wet weather. Perhaps a covey or two had been forced to high ground and might be findable. The land is in Union County, twenty miles south.

I powdered the inside heel of the fourteen-inch Red Balls (now made by LaCrosse with a lifetime guarantee) in anticipation of standing water in the bottoms. Into the truck I hung the 1100 and stashed a box of #9s. I was certain there was no need for more ammo. D.L. was keeping Spook at the old home place, and the big Setter was raring to go. Mack, whom you've seen down east, filled the other box.

Henry Davis, whose My Life as a Hunter early in the century extolled the virtues of "one-man, one-dog," misses the point of quail hunting. Just as it takes two to tango, birdhunting without a partner is unleavened bread. I have been no happier than when you and I, and now D.L. and I, have been out there, with one dog or three.

The territory looked promising indeed, two or three cut bean fields to the left, a huge cut-over to the right (ought to be great next year, too), and a few small lay-outs between beans and road. You always urged me to hunt where beans and cut-over lay adjacent. My heel was hurting, so I elected to range the farm road that split the area.

There was little activity on the perimeter of field one, but as we circled back toward the truck, Spook disappeared on the far side of a two-acre patch of cedar saplings, brush, and broomstraw. As always when a dog is facing the hunters, there is an awkwardness in getting into position. I was then standing in the road, Spook was ahead and to my right, and I could barely see Mack backing on the far edge of the bean field, where D.L. had moved behind Spook. The dogs held like marble statues, but it was obvious that the birds would fly my way and D.L. would get no shot without taking off my head. He simply tossed a rock into the thicket with predictable results. Two flew behind me, the first dead on the ground in twenty yards, but I was too greedy on the second. D.L. said the rest took off directly over my head. For his patience and restraint, I gave thanks. And credited the training of a boy who took his first quail at thirteen under the watchful eye of his dad and old Judge B.

Within the hour, on the roadside of another lay-but, Spook pointed hard, but relocated. Mack had, as usual, circled a running covey and cut them off. But Spook got tangled up in the briars, and D.L. almost stepped on a twelve-bird covey. My #9s caught the first bird across the road, but again I missed the second. That was two for four for me. D.L. turned to take a bird from Mack. His double, falling in the open ground, had obviously run off, because Mack made prodigious efforts to fulfill his promise as a retriever. But a sleeper, bouncing airborne as we left the brush, fell quickly to The Boy's Ithaca pump.

It being now four-thirty or thereabouts on a darkening winter afternoon, and the cut-over too challenging for the late hour, we betook ourselves to another abandoned farm, inherited by one of D.L.'s buddies. He had last week found a covey behind an old barn. This time it was not to be. As we rounded into view, there stood old Mack as you have many times seen a good bird dog—head and tail high, but eyes rolling to the boss: "Hey, man, they got up on me." Spook had gone on ahead around a little pond, and the day was therefore not yet over. The flown covey had pitched in trees as sometimes happens, but on one of these, D.L.'s forty-yard swing shot brought no "dead bird." Mack, however, redeemed himself by bringing in the crip from far down the hill. There were, on cleaning, only three shot in the carcass.

Now four birds in the bag and one left on the ground would certainly not make the papers. But here within a couple of hours we had marked three coveys, taken enough for breakfast, *left seed for another time, and given boy and dad some rare togetherness.*

Oh yes. As we packed it in, he said "Good shootin', Pop."
Fifty percent doesn't really deserve it!

Best,

David

Well, that was written long before this book, but special bird hunts are the stuff of memory.

· 22 ·

Love Affair

---

*E*lsewhere I have profiled some of the fine dogs that hunted with us. I am forced to leave out many. Aside from Spook himself, the protagonist of this effort, space had to be saved for a special lady. Her name, as registered with the Field, was Rebel's Polly Who? The question mark came with the name, affixed before we met by a breeder who obviously expected that she would surprise some folks who might doubt her accomplishments to come.

Spook was at the peak of his powers, but Mack and the others in the kennel were beginning to age, and the boss had developed an insatiable hunger for the sport of quail shooting. So I was on the lookout for a broke dog or dogs to fill in. Bud McCall pointed me to the residence of a fireman in an adjoining county, said to have a pair of Setters, male and female, that were good performers.

I reckoned without background check that the owner would be an easy mark. Not so. He knew what he had, and planned, I'm sure, to take the lawyer from Charlotte, should he want one of those dogs. I never knew whether Bud tipped him off that I was a prospect. When I drove up, he was anything but responsive to my inquiry about a purchase. No, he didn't want to sell a dog. They were the apples of his eye and playmates to his children. They were too good to be turned over to a stranger. His wife would kill him. "But while you're here, let's go look at this little bitch." In retrospect, I don't recall ever being so led down the primrose. I've handled multi-

million-dollar corporate acquisitions where the selling stock-
holders would have lost their shirts to this man. He simply
opened the gate and let loose—how can I say?—Miss Wonderful. Tiny, lightly ticked, tricolored, and with a perfect
Llewellin head, this gal butterflied down the edge of a corn-
field, floated to a frozen point, held until we walked in on a
resident covey. He shot, she retrieved to hand, and I was love-
struck.

Full-broke bird dogs were selling in the Carolinas for
up to two hundred dollars. When I left with her tucked into
the front seat beside me, her head in my lap, my hip pocket
was *four* hundred dollars lighter. For the next twelve hours,
until I could get her into my own bird fields, I knew I had stupidly let down my guard and been thoroughly cheated. Half
an hour after she and Spook nailed the first covey on the
Mobley Place, I knew the fireman had the worst of the deal—
by far. It was ever thus until she left us a decade later. She was
the apogee, the nonpareil, the ultimate in quail dog, and she
and Spook complemented each other in their work as only a
pair melded together by genetic destiny can do.

They quickly formed a team responding to whistle
and hand signal, and, though working down opposite sides of
a hundred-acre bean field, would come about on command or
go inside when indicated. There seemed to be no jealousy on
point, and either would back and honor the first find. Their
ability to locate seemed equal. How could a guy have been
more fortunate for the years they overlapped?

Both were good retrievers, but I made a gross error on
one memorable occasion. Spook had picked up a bird and
brought it in. I found it a bloody mess, and stupidly slapped

him across the muzzle. Too late, I realized that this was a "squealer," too young to have been shot at anyway, and so soft as to have been literally shot to pieces. Never again would Spook come to me all the way, instead dropping every downed bird for me to pick up myself. I still carry that mistake on my conscience.

I deliberately avoided the matter of Polly's breeding for two years. It was out of selfishness, of course, my not wanting to give up hunting her when with pups. However, the obvious promise of a litter out of Polly by Spook was like anticipating a gold strike. Penned together at estrus, she gave him only a couple of snaps, then joined in mutual trust.

The whelping box seemed to run over with the *ten* puppies, although four quickly succumbed to some unsuspected worms thought to have been eliminated in the bitch before birthing. The remaining six I took to the vet, whose big old Basset Hound furnished enough blood for a complete refill on all six.

They grew apace, and, hoping I could fill the kennel with this exclusive breeding, I tried to keep them all. Try teaching six little monsters at a time how to sit, stay, and heel. I was not very successful, despite great help from D.L. Ultimately, two became gun-shy as a result of being taken to the shooting field too soon. One was a true blinker—really birdshy. One, the handsomest Setter male I ever saw, was completely unbiddable, even through three training sessions, including one with Paul Long. Bess won a puppy stakes, and Bullet I gave to my son-in-law Pete. Lost at one point for four years, he recognized his former master, came home, hunted with us for a year or so, and became such a self-hunter that we couldn't use him. What a tragedy that all the experience of the parents, mucked up to a degree by their owner, killed off a great offspring potential.

· 23 ·
Good Reads

You wouldn't be reading this book had you no special feel for dogs, boys, hunting, and the outdoors. Always, there have been writers seeking to capture, in words on paper, the exhilaration we feel when exposed to one or all of the above.

In Spook's day, the greatest of the genre were Robert Ruark, Havilah Babcock, Archibald Rutledge, Burton Spiller, and Dana Lamb. If you have not read them recently, hie yourself to the library and feast.

But all is not lost, and there are a number of fine writers today in the outdoor field. The style of writing has changed with the change of the century. In the nineteenth century, writing was ponderous, overly wordy, highly stylized. By 1920, with the post–World War I style as formulated by Ernest Hemingway, writers began to write more like real people talked.

My current list of favorites by no means includes all the gifted authors I find in reviewing newly published books in my "Bookmarks" column in *Pointing Dog Journal*. The criteria for making the list, however, are pretty severe. I like, in addition to the music involved in the word flow, precision in word use, accurate spelling, consistency in semantics and punctuation. I like descriptive matter that is imaginative but not too purple. I like characters, man or animal, that are defined and real. (Now, having been a bit arrogant, I have hopes for a strong proofreader to hide my own mistakes.) But here are some samples.

From Gene Hill (my own number one) in *Sunlight and Shadows*: "They were both too fat. He had a big safety pin, the kind used for a horse blanket, holding up the front of his hunting coat, and under that an old red-and-green wool shirt that threatened to throw its buttons." You know this man and his old dog from the last field trial.

Or, "Inside there is an old refrigerator, one of those made in a time when everything seemed to run forever, and a plain gray enamel stove that never gave anyone any trouble. An oil-cloth covered table and three mismatched chairs rest on the linoleum floor with the usual buckles in the usual treacherous places; in the corner sits an old armchair with rusted springs coiled like snakes, rescued from the sideyard by someone." Haven't you seen that cabin a hundred times when quail-hunting in the backcountry?

How about Steve Bodio in *A Rage For Falcons*? "And I looked up to see a dot dropping, becoming an inverted heart, a diving bird. The wind screamed through her bells, making a sound like nothing else on earth as she fell a half-mile."

And, "Though we weren't five miles out of town there were magpie nests in the alders, toads trilling in the puddles, ravens diving and croaking, deer tracks in the road. A Cooper's hawk, a haggard with a beautiful blue-gray back and a breast barred with robin-red, worked a contour just above us, alternatively flapping and gliding."

Bill Tarrant, in *How to Hunt Birds With Gun Dogs*, goes back further than most in this collection. But listen: "I was perturbed at the wealth of ducks Scoop presented to me, feeling sorry for the cripples and wanting to pinch the head off the guy who shot and left them, when suddenly, out of the dark, I nearly bumped into an old man who was standing by the dike. He seemed like layered clay, dressed in home-vulcanized waders, a canvas coat out at the elbows, and a grimed cap. He carried a Model 12 shotgun with the barrel worn pewter gray." Now you're bound to know that old man when you see him.

And now, a writer fairly new to me, whom I discovered only a few years ago. I'm a great fan of his Montana, which I have experienced only briefly. In his 1994 *Western Skies,* John Barsness makes the language sing: "The willows grow shorter, mixed with woody forbs, as you crawl farther, and the sand grows wetter. It's all crawl now, the pumpgun held in crossed arms as you walk on thighs and elbows. As you snake through the last bit of covers you see their heads and tails bobbing and rising in the bright brown water, just on the edge of the range—then if you fail to jump up and run in those hot hipboots through the soft, sucking sand to the firm gravel your duck will be half-a-mile down the Missouri before you make it back—."

· 2 4 ·

Yarnspin:
Tales of a Bird-Dog Man

---

*E*very birdhunter, and certainly everybody who doubles as outdoor writer, comes up with a story from time to time in which somebody else is the protagonist. So you seek to record the tale or tales against the day you're doing an article or writing a book. Here are a couple I saved—and even though Spook was not involved, you'll be glad I did.

The death of Colonel Frank Pierson at the Veterans Administration hospital in Salisbury, North Carolina, in early September 1993, marked, as we say, the end of an era. He was recognized with many medals for his army service, but my knowledge of the man was as a bird-dog lover, trainer, breeder, and hunter. His obituary said he was a member of the American Field Hall of Fame, which may have overstated the case. If not, he should have been. He spun lots of yarns around the field-trial circuits, from coast to coast, and dog men have repeated them, but these, to the best of my knowledge, have not had national exposure. Bird-dog lovers deserve, through them, to know the man.

Late in the 1950s, I was hunting quail pretty regularly with a fellow named Cecil Steel down in Union County. Cecil kept dogs of his own and also boarded for others. Among the boarders one season was a small tricolor bitch. I had a mirror-match in my Rebel's Polly Who?, the two being so nearly identical that I could barely tell my own dog. Both were top-flight performers, far better than average. Polly had won some first-place silver, and the other dog was equally good, though I hated to admit it.

Cecil said the visitor belonged to a Colonel Pierson, whom I had met at a field trial or two. He wasn't hunting her that year, which was his loss. Thinking he might not know the true value of his treasure, I schemed to buy her at the end of the season, but when I went back to Steel's, he told me that Pierson had sold her for a *thousand* dollars.

You could probably have bought a young Warhoop Jake for that price in the mid-1950s. I was astounded, and the next time I saw the Colonel I confessed my covetousness and inquired about the dog. "Well," he said, "I'll tell you a story."

"I was going to a field trial in late February at Hoffman. I took Sue to enter the All-Age. Oh, I knew she was that good. It snowed and no one came. I was alone at the clubhouse, making the best of it. The day before, I had hunted Sue and had at least one limit." He smiled. "A big limousine driven by a chauffeur pulled up. In the back was a middle-aged man and, *ahem*, a younger lady. He dismounted in the snow, saw my birds lying out on the table, and wanted to know, 'Is that your dog?' and 'Did she find those birds?' and 'Is she for sale?' I answered yes, yes, and a big *no*. No sale, no price.

"The upshot was that he identified himself as a Mr. Mars, who made candy, and that he would like to rent Sue for the final week at his South Carolina 'plantation,' where the season had another week to go. I thought his credit was good, so I let him use her. Three days into the week Western Union called to say I had a message—and a money order. The message was, 'I bought Sue.' The money order was for an unbelievable one thousand dollars. I cashed it."

On another occasion, by chance also at Hoffman, where the big dogs run, I again bumped into the Colonel. I remember dog prices had really exploded since Sue's day, because the two Flatwood dogs had just brought a reported $40,000. The Colonel was leaving his parked car, and I noticed a sort of off-breed dog left behind. "Colonel," I inquired (I always used the respectful title), "you have just sold two dogs to the Japanese for what's reported as about ten grand each. Why do you have such a mutt for your personal dog?"

Once more he said, "I'll tell you a story." And this is what he told me.

"Not long ago, in early fall, I was leaving Jet, that's the 'mutt,' in the car. Two fellows noted to me that I had left my brake lights on. I looked around, and sure enough the red lights were on. So I thought a minute, and then I said, 'Thanks. I'll have my dog Jet turn them off.' So I whistled through my teeth, and the lights went off, and Jet's head appeared through the back window. You can believe there was some amazement on the faces of those two guys.

"What they didn't know was that on hot days in early fall, Jet would crawl under the dash to get in the shade. When he did, he leaned on the brake pedal, turning on the taillights. When I whistled, Jet jumped up, releasing the pedal, and the lights went out. Simple as that!"

The Colonel is no longer here to spin these yarns himself. I thought I'd do it for him.

Riding Shotgun

I can think back with real appreciation for what a good bird dog means to his boss. There are times, though, when other factors make or break the hunt. Sometimes the dogs are surplus.

My brother Charlie married a girl, Nita, from Surrency, Georgia, which is located, if findable at all, on the banks of the fabled Altamaha River. The area is noted, aside from bluegill fishing par excellence, mostly for pine trees. Great big pine trees, with a high overstory and great quail territory down under: flat piney woods, in the vernacular of the South. Her daddy had several thousand acres that bordered on thousands more timberland owned by International, Weyerhaeuser, and other timber giants. Mr. Tillman, Nita's dad, had hunting access to all of it.

Nita also had brothers and cousins and in-laws by the score, all of whom timbered or farmed, or raised cattle. But there wasn't a bird hunter in the lot! Having heard volumes about the quail population in south Georgia in the mid-1960s, I kept asking Nita, "How's hunting down home?" To which I one day got a welcome reply.

"Well, David," she said, "I've just heard from home, and some of the boys have run into a problem. They wanted me to ask you about it." I knew they didn't need my legal advice, and I was hardly an expert on lumber, farms, or cows. So I was nonplussed. Nita didn't waste much time putting me in the picture. "You know how close we are in Surrency. My uncle's oldest daughter—that's my first cousin, of course—married Harry Wilds, and he's the kinfolks with the problem." She paused, and a little grin appeared.

"Last time we were home, Charlie was telling Harry about how you liked to bird-hunt. That was last summer. Now here it is December, and Harry is hollerin' for help. He said tell you that he wants you to come ride shotgun. Says the quails are attacking him every time he goes to the field, and there's not a bird dog in all of Surrency! Says it hard to drive the Jeep and shoot at the same time, and he needs protection."

Well, I don't mind having my leg pulled in that fashion, so I asked, "When do we leave?" knowing full well she and Charlie must have been planning a trip or the subject would never have come up. The target was the coming week. I cleared the calendar, checked the Sweet Sixteen, oiled my boots, and pronounced myself ready.

My pickup just didn't seem appropriate for the three of us humans on a six-hour ride, so we elected to use Charlie's big station wagon after I assured Nita that Spook and Mack were gentlemen and car-broke. Accordingly, two large cardboard boxes, with one side of each cut out for entry, were placed behind the backseat well stacked with coastal Bermuda hay and two all-white dogs. Who promptly curled up and went to sleep, requiring only two roadside relief stops as we passed through South Carolina.

Cousin Harry ran some farming operations that required his attention hands-on in the field. When I was there, one of the chores was controlled burning of woodlands on the place. But the operation was in good hands, so Harry said,

"Let's hunt!" Now here's where the surprise came. Except for retrieving, we hardly needed the two Setters. Harry drove up to within fifty yards of every covey. And there were ten of them, if I recall, that first day. More birds than I had seen in seasons: well-feathered, healthy bobwhites seemingly just waiting for the Jeep to pull up and off-load its shotgunners before flying into the flat woods not then being burned. That gave us a few singles, but we really didn't hunt much besides coveys, so the dogs picked up birds to hand and we moved on.

It was a pleasant interval, with kin-in-laws I'd never met, some beautiful territory, fine food, and birds "like they used to be." Can you remember seeing one hundred fifty birds a day? I thought you might like to think back to the 1960s, if you're old enough, or believe I'm lying if you're not.

· 26 ·
Coda

*T*hree times before have I actually written eulogies for departed dogs—all special, all dear friends. All of them came after Spook. Each time, when Polly, Kate, and Brandt the Lab, died, I cried big tears, real tears. With Polly, blind and toothless, I could not bear to turn her over to the vet's needle, and I lovingly put the .32 into the ear of my trusting darling and eased her pain—but not mine. Kate developed a swiftly moving cancer and suffered only briefly. Brandt, the housedog shared with Maxine, went at the soft hands of Dr. Baron, who had taken the beat-up old arthritis-racked body from my arms while I blindly walked back to the truck and sobbed all the way home. The newspaper story about Brandt's passing created quite a stir. Calls came from distant places, memorials were tendered, replacement pups rejected with thanks.

I am not at this late date going soft in bidding goodbye to Spook on paper. That does not mean I loved him any less. And to use any word less strong than "love" would be to denigrate the relationship. We had a mutual respect for almost fifteen years. In the last two years of his life he was restricted to the kennel, yipping his displeasure at being left behind, and then yipping his welcome when we returned. In the field when he was about thirteen, he began to ignore calls and whistles, obviously from growing deafness. When he could no longer find me or the truck, I would walk him down and lead him in. So his hunting days were over, and he was relegated to his pen with the big juniper dog box that had been exclusively his for his lifetime.

Came the inevitable day when, just at dark on a January evening, after fourteen full years, there was, at the hunting truck's return, no answering yip.

I found him in his box as though he had gone peacefully to sleep, the long white body stretched full length. The old heart had stopped, and I was bereft.

In the deep black soil adjacent to the kennel runs, under the walnut tree that had shaded his run in summer, I plunged the shovel. But first, I held up a wet finger, as I had so often done when putting out on a hunt with him. The wind was from the west. To the west I laid him, nose into the wind, just as he always ran.

Books Mentioned in Spook and Other Stories

Argue, Denny. *Pointers and Setters*. London: Swan Hill, 1993.

Babcock, Havilah. *Tails of Quail and Such*. Columbia, SC: University of South Carolina, 1951.

Barsness, John. *Western Skies*. New York: Lyons & Burford, Publishers, 1994.

Bodio, Steve. *A Rage for Falcons*. New York: Lyons & Burford, Publishers, 1984.

Brown, William F. *Field Trials*. Chicago: American Field Publishing, 1987.

Fergus, Charles. *Gun Dog Breeds*. New York: Lyons & Burford, Publishers, 1992.

Griffin, Jeff. *Hunting Dogs of America*. Garden City, NY: Doubleday, 1964.

Hill, Gene. *Sunlight and Shadows*. New Albany, OH: Countrysport, 1995.

Hochwalt, A.F. *Bird Dogs: Their History and Achievement*. London: The Sportsman's Press, 1922.

King, Alfred, Sr. *The Llewellin Setter*. Conway, AR: self-published, 1992.

Laverack, Edward. *The Setter*. London: C.W. Sorensen, 1872.

Pass, Aaron. "Dixie Bird Dog." Des Moines, IA: *Pointing Dog Journal*, 1993.

Rutledge, Archibald. *Hunting and Home in the Southern Heartland*. Edited by Jim Casada. Columbia, SC: University of South Carolina Press, 1992.

Tarrant, Bill. *How to Hunt Birds with Gun Dogs*. Mechanicsburg, PA: Stackpole Publishing, 1994.

Tuck, Davis. *The New Complete English Setter*. Charlottesville, VA: Howell Press Inc., 1982.